ONCE UPON A TIME THERE WAS NO MONEY

By

Joseph Clark

Once Upon a Time There Was No Money
Copyright© 2004 by Joseph Clark
No part of this book may be reproduced or transmitted in any form or by any means, graphic, electronic or mechanical, including photocopying, recording, typing, or by any information storage retrieval system, without the permission of the publisher.
For information:
New Energy Books
P.O. Box 6471
Broomfield, Co 80021
First Printing 3/2005
Revised Edition 6/2005
ISBN 0-9770535-0-4
Printed in the United States of America

ONCE UPON A TIME THERE WAS NO MONEY

WHAT YOU NEVER THOUGHT MONEY WAS ABOUT

BOOK ONE OF THE EVOLUTION SERIES
A Shaumbra Book

CONTENTS

Credits	xiii
Forward	i
Overview	iii
And So the Story Begins	**1**
Class Begins	3
Chapter One	**8**
Money	9
Test	22
Wars	23
Tags	24
Chapter Two	**26**
How Things Were Done & The Reality	27
of That Time Era	27
The System	27
Part Two Banks	36
Money what good is it?	38
The Bankers Manifesto of 1892	39
Two Faces Of A Loan Transaction	40
Chapter Three	**48**
Expectations of a new era	49
Psychological effects	50
Education	51
Housing	52
Science	52
People	53
Law	53
Justice	55
Chapter Four	**58**
Education & Transformation	59
Future	59
Transportation	60
Communications	61
Security	62
Freedoms	66
Medical	67
Recycling Technology	68
Supply and Demand	69
Health	71
Religion	72
Critics	73
Chapter Five	**76**
Class Review Chapter Three & Four	77

Chapter Six **100**
    Evolution of the Human and the Soul 101
    The New Earth 105
    Beliefs, a point of view 106
    Travel 106
    Spiritual Groups Are they really all that 106
    spiritual 106
    Disconnect 107
    Feeling 110
    Thoughts 111
    Multi Dimensional Thinking 112
    The Journey of a True Lightworker 112

Chapter Seven **114**
    Future Lifestyle 115
    Marriage & Relationships 115
    Love, what is it? 115
    Products 118

Chapter Eight **136**
    The Higher Understandings and Aspects 137
    of the Coming Times Just Ahead 137
    Karma 137
    Church 140
    Change 141
    Some public changes 141
    Peace 143

Chapter Nine **162**
    How things really work on earth and in 163
    the higher realms 163
    Science Revisited 163
    Indigo Children 165
    Changing Times 165
    Biology Bubbles 166

Chapter Ten **172**
    The Power of True Belief 173
    Money! What good is it? 174
    True Power of Belief Continued 177
    Tool for Changing Beliefs 178
    To Sum It Up 186
    Authors Closing Comments 188
    A Backup Plan 189

Credits

I must give credit to all who have helped me or at times have forced me along my life path to the understandings that brought me to the writing of this book. There have been many different situations and experiences both up and down that belong to the understanding in this book. I must be honest and say since I live in the money era I have written this book partly for the money; however, what is most important here is that I have also written this book for the future evolution of humanity. In publishing this information, I have done a small part in service to the whole of humanity's evolution. So credit goes out from here into the future men and women that use this information to better their lives and the lives of others. In addition credit must also go to the invisible helpers that made the word flow onto the pages as I was allowed to connect to a higher source of wisdom.

JC

Forward

The information in this book is based on *probable future potentials*. The history discussed here is fact and is in no way a complete recall of any or all the facts from the current past time period of history. These facts are an overview of some of the strong points of the time pertaining to money. The future discussed in this book is a potential scenario of what may be. Since the future is not written until we live it, it can only be predicted based on our current mindsets and the strongest potential before us now in order to predict a probable potential path. It is difficult to be accurate because there are many sets of multiple potentials that spring out in many different directions. The most likely future potentials based on our current perceptions of reality are written about in this book.

This book was written to offer an alternative to the way life has evolved in our present MONEY reality. MONEY encompasses everything in our lives. Because of this money and the control placed upon us by ourselves where we allow others and this money to be the deciding factor in everything we do. Today it has become so bad that it is impossible to know whom one can trust. Remember early history, the American Indians did not use money. They lived very peacefully until they started to trade with other tribes using an equal value for equal value system, and particularly when trading with the white man. After that, their lifestyle was ripped apart. Since money is the root of all evil as we all know, it only makes sense to get rid of it for a better way of life where everyone will be living for his or her personal growth rather than always striving just to maintain a sense of balance in ones life. This book shows a progression from the mundane life of the 20th century to the not-so-mundane future life of a people sometime in the 23rd century. The perspective presented is a view from the present looking forward to the 23rd century, which is in turn looking back on the 20th century as their history lessons. If you are reading this book, you most likely are looking for some kind of change in your personal life and reality.

Energy is nothing more than a dormant potential. This energy is only realized by the choices made in ones word. The potential of money is an energy that's potential has been distorted by mixed and dark energies and choices choice's of many dark souls and has gone awry. It now lacks its most positive and beneficial outcome of all the possibilities in the world of man.

This book is not about attracting money, but there is a tool in this book that may help do just that. Instead, this book is about the true abundance of existence and the universal truths, which can only come when MONEY is abolished from circulation. Money is not really true abundance~it is *only money* or a tangible substance and energy people have placed a value on. This energy is highly restricted by the values we have place upon it, due to greed, control from others in control of this money and the hoarding nature of these corrupt individuals values. The real true abundance comes automatically when having to trade one thing for another stops. True abundance is a state of being where all things on earth are free of exchange of money or trade of goods that people have placed a value on. Does the sun require anything from the planets it warms? No. It just is. And it simply shines its light and warmth to all in its path. It's only the minds of people that require an exchange of some kind. There is a reason for this hoarding and taking and placing value on things that stems from a time of separation of our souls from "The All That Is" during a time very long ago that has to do with how we came into being in this universe. I will not tell that story so there is no confusion about the purpose of this book. Because money is so desired, required, and demanded by all it creates, hatred to grow toward others when the money that is expected is withheld.

Overview

The creation of money is a restriction on people who otherwise would have no such restrictions. It causes greed and oppression on all people, but mostly it affects the weaker people when the strong afflict their misuse of money upon the weak. When limitation, control, oppression, and scarcity occur as a result of a lack of money, the free soul after a period of time no longer tolerates it and rebels to some degree', depending on how much pressure is brought to bear at any given time. This rebelling has caused some chaos, which has led the strong or the controllers to create rules (*laws* as they later became to be known) and force them onto the weaker people. At the very beginning of this rule-generating time, it seemed to be a good thing to have rules and control. Because the people of that very early time were totally uneducated and somewhat barbaric, the rules brought some ease to the weaker people that were being taken advantage of by the strong.

In time this all changed—the rules created a hierarchy and the strong and rich fed off the weak despite the rules. They even moved into a place where they could use the rules in their favor to further oppress the week. This oppressing the weak occurred over a long period of time, so the weak didn't notice it so easily. Over time the strong made the laws seem not so bad to the weak, as they moved in small but steady steps to slowly take total control of everything. Much like one learns in science class about boiling a frog slowly, most likely it progressed so slowly that no one could see where it was going to end up. The strong were the best fighters in the groups and the weak knew they would lose if they rose up against the strong. This continued for more centuries than can be counted until the time of writing this book, it most likely will continue for some time yet to come. It is unknown for sure how much longer this will continue. There will be at least two more generations to come before we see an end to this era of money, and the control we allow upon us by its use.

This prediction is based on the new generations of people being born now that will be even greater victims of the current system. This new generation is different intellectually and will not abide by the same restrictions as past generations have. This is evidence of our evolution in action here. In times past, the strong enlisted the not-so-weak and trained them to carry out instructions to help control others for them.

Much later in time they were called *police*.

The early system of *trade* and *barter* was good before the advent of money. Money came in during the later stages of trade and barter as a means of convenience when a person did not have any goods of value to trade for the goods one needed. Early man hoarded food for the cold winters that they knew would come each season. From lack of goods came the start of the idea of swapping something one had plenty of with another that had plenty of what was desired or needed. This grew into trading, which grew into a lack of things to trade, which grew into the invention of money: a convenient, equitable commodity all could us as a tool of trade when goods were not readily available for trading. The appearance of money created the elevated levels of merchant traders, which led to arguing over possessions and so on. The creation of money led to the feeling of unfair trading between parties, which led to the creation of a policing type control over the trading. The attitude of trade was that one possessed what one created, killed, or grew on the land. Trading was done by a means of fair value for fair value. When money was created, it complicated this value of trade.

Although the intentions behind creating money were innocent enough, in the end the strong took advantage of the weak and are still doing so today in greater measure than ever before--like a disease. This is a simplistic overview of the creation of money, but events generally transpired along these lines over time. In time the strong became more educated. When they realized they could control all other people in all types of trading by the use of money, they had a way to take total control over everything and everyone --all they had to do was get control of the money. By controlling the money itself they could control all other things. At that point in time during the early days, money appeared in the form of gold and silver. Things all changed drastically in the late 1800's and early 1900's when the smart and powerful few finally figured out a way to take over the entire world through the use of money. They knew they couldn't control the hard currency very well since it had been in circulation for so long and their plan would not work with only a limited supply of gold and silver. It is currently impossible to make gold from nothing, so to make their plan work they had to remove it from circulation and replace it with soft currency (paper money), which could be made in unlimited quantities for next to nothing. I will explain this more in later chapters, but for now you get the idea of the very ancient history of man and trade up to the time of this book. One cannot trust anyone else as long as people are using any means of value for value trade; this is especially true where money is used in the trading.

In present time we have an evolved sense of MONEY as being a very controlling factor in our mental, emotional and physical world, with total control by the banking and government systems of the day. The control led to laws and more laws and more laws—so many laws that they need enormous rooms to keep these law books in. These laws have been rebelled against for, as long as there have been laws and control. This is a vicious cycle of law and rebellion. In the time of writing this book, there is the saying that you cannot fight the system. Of course that saying was created by the system to instill fear in those that may try to fight or rebel against it. They went to such lengths to instill fear in the masses that they would imprison some people for years and then highly publicize that they did so, in an effort to instill fear that they knew would keep others from trying to fight or upset their system. Fear is their way of doing business and controlling others.

This vicious cycle is one where no one really wins, not even the system. For now you get the idea of what things must have been like in this system of existence to the students of our class as we will be looking back from the perspective of the 23rd century. From this book you will start to get the idea of what money can do to a free soul. We will get deeper into the facts later on in other chapters. I will give a comparison later of the differences of a money society and a non-money society. A free human soul will not be controlled or oppressed for very long. Life always finds a way to free itself from most anything.

A small government will still exist, but it will be in no way like the one of the money era. It will be more of a teaching government that helps people share knowledge and technologies all over the world. Each national government will be a contact point for other countries and will be a source of information for all throughout the World Net system of what is now called the Internet. There will no longer be any red tape like that which exists in the current money era. There will no longer be any kind of government control over the individual person at any level.

v

What we as people believe has a direct and profound bearing on our lives and the way everything progresses in a society. We create what we believe. Many beliefs are passed down from earlier generations so they tend to live on for the next generation even though they are outdated. The good news is that each generation will alter the old teachings to some degree or may discard them altogether. The power of belief is more powerful than a raging locomotive. What a person believes on the deepest levels makes all the difference in every area of existence. There will be more information about the power of belief in later chapters near the end of this book.

As you read this book you will find repetitiveness at times from chapter to chapter and within the same chapter from the narrative to student comments. It is my intention to be repetitive due to the importance of learning and holding this information in your mind like a TV commercial or a song. My wish is to deeply imbed this information into your subconscious mind because it is time for change.

AND SO THE STORY BEGINS

Not so very long ago, an age of people lived in a society where they used money as a means of trading with each other and they thought it was good. In this era there were many, many horrible things that occurred because of the use of money, but they didn't know that this money was the actual cause of so many atrocities in their lives. They had a government that employed the brightest minds in the world in science, engineering, medicine, sociology, and many other areas, and they knew that money was what they called the "root of all evil" in the world. Yet, the greed and desire to control the world was so great in the people that ran the government, they could not see that they needed to get rid of money in order to create peace. This would be the answer to all of the major problems in the world.

Money is an energy source. This energy can be highly beneficial to all or it can be devastating to all--it all depends on how it is used. In their day it was used to control and enslave the population of earth.

In this system they would be able to control people by changing prices on merchandise and services in any way they wanted to, because cost along with the amount of money a person had, determined the quality of life a person could achieve or be confined to. Let me take you on a journey into the future and then we will turn around and look back at the past and we will investigate this system and uncover the way people lived for possibly hundreds of centuries. In this journey we will witness a class of young people discovering there past heritage. So without further ado, let's delve into the future classroom of Ms. Alison and her High School students located in Aston Pennsylvania. What better place to visit than Pennsylvania, as this is the birthplace and seat of our U.S. history?

When we get rid of money we will all become equal and we will all become extremely wealthy because the use of money is a controlling factor that keeps us in servitude to another's will. When we are in servitude, we are not free, with a limited amount of money we are not considered equal, and we are limited in wealth by the amount of money others allow us to have (control). After the removal of money, we become wealthy because the earth is extremely abundant and all of her abundance is there for our taking without cost or any requirements imposed upon us by the earth. There is nothing on this earth that is not free to us as the custodians of the planet.

From the moment each child is born into the current world system(s) of thinking we currently have, a conditioning of the mind immediately comes into play from all the prior people and their mind set that came before the child. This preset consciousness causes a perpetuation of the same ways of life upon each new generation. Seeing things from a fresh new perspective that is without the old ways of thinking frees us to be able to engage a completely new way of looking at our present day self and the circumstances that are so controlling over each of us. This is of course by our own creation and permission by mental conditioning that seems to be unchangeable in the system of the present day because it is so ingrained in us from birth that makes us all think we need money to live. We also think we will die if we do not have this money. Those minds that are in this type of thinking were taught by their parents and elders, which were also from a state of need for the necessities of life that are or may have been withheld and or controlled by a total lack of or by a shortened supply of money. This scenario is directly related to control and fear perpetrated by the workings of the governmental systems in place at any given time through history and of course in the present day. This is where the lazier greedier power hungry people gravitate to so they can live easily off the rest of the population without ever lifting a finger to help anyone other than themselves.

Class Begins

Ms. Alison:
Hello, class, I am Ms. Alison. Welcome to the first day of the new school year.

In case you were wondering, this class is Sociology History. Please make sure you intended to take this class, please check your class schedules. I wouldn't want to teach you something you didn't want to know about.

Before we begin does anyone have any questions?......... We will be studying history and the use of money. Our studies will delve into the usage and psychological effects of this substance called money.

Bill:
Ms. Alison?

Ms. Alison:
Yes, Bill, do you have a question?

Bill:
Yes, I do. You called it a substance that caused psychological effects--did they eat this stuff?

Ms. Alison:
No, Bill, they did not eat it. We will delve into the facts about this substance and what it did to them and how it did it a little later on.

I have pulled a book from the library archives that will be the main study guide for this class. A book called *Once Upon A Time There Was No Money*, with the subtitle "What You Never Thought Money Was About".
This book is on your schoolbook memory cards. Please slip your cards into your desk station readers and pull up this book. Turn to the overview and we will get started.
This book was written by a man that lived in the latter part of this era of money. He was a forward visionary thinker for his time. In fact he wrote in this book of a classroom in the future just like this one that was learning exactly what we will discover in our class studies of this past era in our present time. This is the main reason I chose this as our study guide.

I will start off by reading to you the section entitled "And So the Story Begins" from the beginning of the book.

[Ms. Alison reads this section to the class.]

Ms. Alison addresses the class:
So, class, that begins our discussion for the year. If you haven't read the forward and overview, I would like you to read this sometime before tomorrow's class to get acquainted with the premise of this book. I would like to discuss the beginning of this subject by asking you for your comments on how much you understand about money and the ways they used it to control people back in this era.

Nebb:
Ms. Alison?

Ms. Alison:
Yes, Nebb.

Nebb:
From what I know, I am under the impression that they lived a very structured life. I mean they had to have a *job* as they called it and they were required to work about eight hours out of every day without exception except for the weekends. They were only allowed to take a very short vacation once per year and that was only allowed when their boss would let them take the time off for this vacation. My grandmother says they would sometimes lose that vacation time if the job required that they be on the job under certain circumstances or they sometimes were forced to only take the time off at inconvenient times of the year. She says these jobs are where they earned this money from. She also says that to earn money was to work for so many hours per week and then the job would give them some money in exchange for the hours they worked. At least that is what grandma says.

Ms. Alison:
Yes, Nebb, that is true, some people would lose their time off if they didn't take it when the company said they could. They sometimes would get paid extra and sometimes not by the company they worked for, but that was all up to the company. As for the money again yes they would work many hours in exchange for the money the company would give them each week or so.

Ms. Alison:
Let's get to the sections I read you. Does anyone have any comments on that?

Lelan:
I do, Ms. Alison.

Ms. Alison:
Tell us what you think.

Lelan:
Actually I have a comment on the forward page about the probable potentials, I see that we do live just that way. There are many options we can choose at any given time. I think a good understanding of this helps us to make better decisions in our daily lives. It requires us to think before we act so that we don't make a really bad mistake that we would regret later. Pertaining to this book we could have developed an entirely different society than we did and maybe that would have been really bad for us all. I wonder if this book had anything to do with the way things did work out. How many people read this and did it make a difference?

Ms. Alison:
We may never know the answer to that, Lelan. It sound like you have read the beginning of this book?

Lelan:
Yes Ms. Alison I have because I wanted to get a start on our lessons to know something about the topic of study.

Ms. Alison:
Has anyone else read the first pats of this works?

[Class all raises their hands signaling they have read the beginning pages before class started.]

Ms. Alison:
Does anyone else have a comment on the beginning of this book?

Karen:
We must be living like the American Indians, because they did not use money

either.

Ms. Alison:
Yes, Karen, that could be surmised from this.

Karen:
I can see how the restrictions can cause so many problems like the creation of policing and laws and all that stuff, but I am still a little confused about the rest of this era. Maybe we should move on to the rest of the book to learn more?

Ms. Alison:
Yes, Karen, I think since you are all wondering about this money, we should go forward and read the next chapter to understand a bit more about this time in our history. I will read the next chapter now.

Chapter One

Money
Ms. Alison reads:
Money is a real killer of souls. Through restriction, it creates lack, the system creates need for money, and that in turn creates desire in the people. It kills the mind by creating corruption of the mind, which infects the soul and ultimately destroys the individual even though the person may not think there is anything wrong with his or her life. Proof of this comes when money is taken away--the addiction to it and the seizures start to surface just the same as when a drug addict goes into withdrawal. Think about your life. If money were taken away but the need for it still prevailed (i.e. bills and money to buy food, clothing etc.), what would you be experiencing then?

Money is nothing more than paper that people have placed a value on by placing our own energy into it. We have put so much of our thoughts, energy and trust into it that it has seemingly taken on a life of its own. We all clamber for it in ever-greater quantities. It appears to give us a sense of stability and peace when we obtain it. What we are actually doing is drawing on the energy of others that also clamber for the same money we have obtained. This is a vicious circle where we as a people have put all our trust and energy into an inanimate object and then we worship it as we might worship an idol in a church in the form of a cross or statue. By doing this, there are many negative things we do not realize, which we are actually doing directly to ourselves. First, by what we are taught we fall to a depth where we think money is a Godsend and if we have a lot of it, we think and even feel it makes us a better person, this is a draw on the energy of money others and ourselves have placed in the money. From this perspective, we do not realize or see that we are inundated with the negative effects of what using money really does to us. Those effects are a dependency on the false energy we ourselves placed in this money as we hoped and thought would be a positive energy for us when we get money. It is an invisible energy that we cannot see, realize or understand what it or (we) are doing to ourselves by continuing to use this false energy of money or an energy of others. We also do not see how to get out of this energy bubble either. We just think we must continue to deal with the use of this type of energy, this is because of the constant bringing forth of old mindsets of our parents and ancestors. We can always get out of this type of understanding with a little freethinking and a change in our way of understanding on how humans and the world can coincide with each other. This existence would be far easier and far more harmonious when we remove our energy from money and take back our own personal power that we have placed in this money. We have also allowed all the dark and misguided souls to control this energy and thus we allow them to control us as well by our own continued belief in and need for the use of money.

Seeing things from a fresh new perspective can give us an easy means to circumvent the old outmoded ways that use control and deceit for continuing the muddied systems of our thinking. Looking at ourselves through the eyes and the minds of a future generation that no longer uses money, will give us a perspective and new way of thinking that will bring us out of the current ways of oppression. It will eliminate the control from all the banks and systems of government and it will free us from the pressures of a "must do or go without and be deprived" way of thinking and treating others and most importantly ourselves. From the perspective of the minds of this future generation that can be found in the book entitled "Once Upon A Time There Was No Money", we can see how easy it is for us to exist and even prosper in new ways in our minds, our world, and our hearts. This allows us to be free from the oppressions created by man especially the greedy ones that try so hard to take the energy of money from others. When we take back our power from the energy of money we also cut off the dark souls that seek to control everything on the planet to be in service to them. I.E. Governments, Banks, the controlling type of employers with threats of a loss of income from your job, and other types of institutions that would have you bow to their demands. You can likely come up with a list of your own in this regard. As long as we continue to use the money that is controlled by the banks and governments, we are allowing them to continue to control us in all the negative ways they are treating all of us.

Money takes away one's true freedom and enslaves one to the effects of the drug called money. This drug is only effective when two or more people use it between each other. The cure is to *stop taking it*. Only at that point will people revert back to a healthy state of mind and soul. When groups of people stop using this drug, others that continue to be addicted will soon follow along because they will see the freedom that removing money creates in others and they will see it can also be created in themselves. They will want to be free of the addiction and control this drug enslaves them into. This will spread very fast once it starts. This is not like using bartering at all. Bartering, is a form of trade that is similar to what was discussed earlier, it only leads back to money. That is why bartering is not very popular and is seldom used. Bartering would only lead one, as it does now, back to the use of money.

The creation of money was likely done with good intent and was thought to be good for all. What they didn't realize was where it would eventually lead society. And rightly so–how could they possibly have seen that far ahead? I cannot believe that it was planned from the beginning to harness and control other people.

[Ms. Alison finishes reading and directs her own comments to the class.]
Students, you know that you can travel around this world and do as you wish whenever you wish with no restrictions. Sally, when I saw you in the grocery store just last week you told me that you and Margaret are going to Switzerland on a skiing trip during the winter season while class is still in session. You all know that there are no restrictions on any of you, so you can do anything you want whenever you want. It was not that way in the past. First there was the restriction on what was called a *minor* to travel around the world, and then there was a restriction from the parents to go and do something like skiing in Switzerland, especially if you lived in the USA. Then there was the biggest restriction of all, the amount of money it would take to get to Switzerland and all the costs of food and lodging for a stay there. If you did not have a lot of this money, you were not likely to make this skiing trip in your lifetime. Money caused so many restrictions that few people ever traveled, or ever did much of anything for that matter. Only the very rich could move about the world easily. This was all because of money.

Sally, you know you can resume your education when you get back, you can follow this class with your communication unit, or you can go to school in Switzerland if you decide to stay there for any length of time. Again, there is no restriction in our society as there used to be in the era of money. You all know that you are only asked to help out and do something now and then to support the whole of our system. I would like to give another example of the past and compare that to today; in fact, this will be an assignment in the next few days of class.

[Ms. Alison continues reading.]
People would buy cars, homes, and clothes, and so on, and they would live with these things for a very long time in some cases. This was because they could not afford to buy new items when the ones they had wore out or broke down. This was again a restriction of money and this was based on their station or class in life. During this time, this was created and maintained by the design of the strong and rich people who molded the system the way they

wanted it to be. They made sure the majority of people had little money due to low wages and they made the cost of things just high enough so that people were tied to a job to make just enough money to pay for the high-priced things. This system was meant to keep people occupied with steady work rather than permit them time to think about or question the authority they lived under. This took years in many cases to pay for necessities. The rich did this so the average people would spend most of their time working just to be able to maintain a mediocre lifestyle while hardly ever getting ahead. The rich lived well of the rest of the people under this system. This kept them from asking questions about why things were the way they were. Many people would force themselves to drive very old beat-up and worn out cars because of the class they lived in. Some would wear the same clothes for years without getting new ones. Others would look down on them as a lower class of people. This was especially done by the upper class and the super rich classes of people. This was a very stressful way of existing and most that were forced into this "lower" class would become angry and some even violent toward their fellow citizens. They would sometimes steel from others because of this lack and the control. Lack of money never lessened the need for money. People were even murdered because of the stress money placed on the people to such a heavy degree.

[Ms. Alison quits reading.]

Ms. Alison:
Crandall?

Crandall:
Yes, Ms. Alison.

Ms. Alison:
I want you to read this next section to the class. This is a partial list of material things that no longer exist because money is no longer used in society.

Crandall:
Money
Banks
Large oppressive governments
Boundaries between countries

Police that would arrest you because they didn't like the way you looked
Lawyers
Taxes
Bookkeepers

Ms. Alison, what is a lawyer? And what are taxes?

Ms. Alison:
We will cover that a little later, Crandall. Please continue with the list.

Crandall:
Judges
Crime
Theft
Bills
Courts
Jails
Hundreds of thousands of people in jails
Excessive laws and the control that came with the laws
No more oppression of new technologies that can benefit all
Hunger
Basic needs not being met for all people
Homeless people
Force against the free will of people
Insurance companies
Military and wars
City, county & state agencies
Stockbrokers
Casinos
Lotteries
Credit reports
Bad commercials on TV and radio
The IRS

Ms. Alison:
Thank you, Crandall

Ms. Alison:
Simon... I want you to read this next section to the class. This is a list of emotional things that no longer exist because money is no longer used.

Simon:
Stress and mental duress
Oppression by others
All crime that dealt with money, which is most all types of crime
Restrictions on being whatever you want to be and going wherever you want to go
Lack of education
Force to keep a person in a situation one may not desire
Neediness
Desire for a better life
Envy
Power over others

Jimmy:
Ms. Alison?

Ms. Alison:
Yes, Jimmy

Jimmy:
Ms. Alison, I am only 16 but I cannot ever remember being told that I could not have or achieve anything in my life ever. So you mean that those people were controlled by money. How could it do that? I don't understand. It was only made of paper, wasn't it?

Ms. Alison:
Well, Jimmy, I don't mean the money itself controlled the people. It was the greed of the people using it and the needs for it that were set up for money by that society. They were then able to control others due to their neediness for money. You see, they thought that using money was good for such a long time that it became deeply ingrained in their society that it was a good system and thus they became dependent upon acquiring it. Because of their dependency on money everyone strived to get as much of it as possible so they could do what they called *having a better quality of life.*

You see, Jimmy, there were different levels of life then- as mentioned earlier they separated themselves on levels they called *classes* of people. There was the lower class, which had little or no money then, there was the middle class that had what was called a *fair income* from the jobs they worked and they lived a very controlled life. The middle class was also known as the working class. They were the ones that did most of the work in their world. Then there was the upper middle class who made more money and worked less than the middle class did. They controlled the middle class to a great degree. Then there was the upper class that made more money than the other classes and they controlled both lower classes even more than the other two classes did. Then there were the super rich. By the word *rich* it was meant that you had a great deal of money. And they controlled everything below them in every way. Being rich in that era meant that others placed a great deal of respect upon the rich person. Everyone wanted to be like the rich so they could do as they pleased when they pleased. This money enabled them to do as they wished easily in there era.

The upper class was never satisfied with just having a lot of this money and control over what was called the *masses of people*, so they also strived to gain even more control over even more of the world. The government of that time, which also exerted its control through money, was a very big controller of everyone. Within this government there were some very corrupt and controlling individuals that had all the power. These people were never heard from by the masses. They hid behind politics, banks, and numerous corporations to keep their identities from being revealed. They had to keep from being exposed or they would be killed by the masses.

Gail:
Ms. Alison?

Ms. Alison:
Yes, Gail.

Gail:
I am sure glad I did not live back then--it sounds horrible.

Ms. Alison:
Yes, Gail, it was, but the people did not know it was. As you remember, I said they were very deeply submerged in the belief that this was how the world was run for a very long period of time and they thought it was going to continue that way forever. They believed that the way out of the control and oppression was to make a lot of money; however, this only made them slaves to the

money and control even more as they gained more money. The lower classes were slaves both to money and the rich. But the rich became slaves to their own money. We already know that money was energy, this energy over time had taken on such a mystique it seemed to have a life of its own. Having a lot of it meant you had to guard it viciously from others taking it away from you. The government of the time perpetuated this slavery to money because they liked to have control and thought it was necessary. The government would play the people like a game. After all, if they had no money they too would have to work for a living, meaning they would have to earn money to survive by getting a real job rather than sitting in the cushy positions where they bossed others around and took their money for any reason they chose. This was always for no real good reason. Remember, they had to have money to be able to go to the store and bring home food, clothing, and necessities and they even exchanged money for housing and cars. In fact, to pay for a house and a car would take most of the money they earned, especially the housing. Buying a house could take as long as 30 years of earnings to pay for. These government people were greedy, lazy, and used to getting money for nothing and were not about to become working class citizens.

All of this is what locked the people of that era into a job. The people that had the jobs often felt it was a heavy burden on their mental and emotional conditions.

Greg:
Ms. Alison, what exactly is a *job*?

Ms. Alison:
Greg, it is the same thing we do today that we call *helping the social structure of life*. What we do today is to volunteer to help get things done that need to be done, such as maintaining the roads for everyone to travel on. Back then it was done in a much different way. The government supervised the work of maintaining roads. They would get together and plan a new road or the maintenance of an existing road, and then they would look to see if they had the money to pay for it, and then if they didn't have the money, they would go to the public and ask for the money. If they did not get the money that way and they really wanted to build this road, they would raise taxes that the people would have to pay even if they disagreed with the road or with the concept of paying taxes, which was then forced upon them. Sometimes they would borrow the money and build the road, then charge a toll to use the

road. All of this further burdened the people and their money supply even further. The average family had very little money because they had to give most all of it away to buy food, clothes, housing, cars, fuel for the cars and so on. On top of that they were forced to pay from one quarter to three quarters of their money in income taxes to the government. Life in general was a very burdensome task to undertake for the largest portion of the population.

Getting back to the roads–they would hire people that knew about building roads and pay them money to build or maintain them. This is all unlike what we do today to take care of our roads. Some of you know Mr. Kelly's wife, Sally. She takes care of the roads for our local community from Aston to McKenzie. All she needs to do is get a call from a citizen or the road inspectors who examine the road conditions and if there is a problem with one of our roads, she will call any road people she knows to make the repairs. They then gather others that have the knowledge and experience to do these kinds of repairs and the road will be repaired. If there are no road repair people available because they have moved to some other part of the country as so many people do, she will call the radio and TV stations and they will run an add for the new road people that may be in the listening area to come and volunteer to repair an existing road or build a new one. As you all know, this requires no money at all to do.

It was different than the way we do things today, back then it was called a *job*. Many people kept the same job all their lives.

Phil:
Ms. Alison?

Ms. Alison:
Yes, Phil.

Phil:
How could someone keep the same job all his or her life? Isn't that a real bore?

Ms. Alison:
Phil, I do know some people today that love what they do now so much that they will most likely do it for their entire lives. Just look at our librarian, Mr. Wents. He has always loved books and spreading knowledge to others so much that he has been in this position for 67 years. I am sure he will continue

until he will no longer be able to help out in that way. His service to all other humans has been the same for his whole life. As you already know many others only do a service for a year or two, then go, and learn a new service to help the needs of the people, but many do not.

Andrew:
Ms. Alison, can you tell us about those taxes?

Ms. Alison:
Andrew, that is a very big subject but I guess it is time to explain a little about that. Some kings created taxes way back in the early days of the noble's and king's era. I won't go into all that today, but for now I will say it was a way for the government to gather up money and control the people in the way the government wanted to control them. I will touch on taxes in a discussion at another time.

How many of you are unaware of our simpler rules of today? And of the fact that we do not force anything on others against their free will. No one. Good. I am glad to see you understand our principles of life today.

However, class, I wish to go over in part the things that we do have today that stand in strong opposition to this past era of study.

Our rules are very simple today.
We have gone back to a biblical time and brought forward the age-old saying, "Do unto others as you would want them to do unto you," and
We have incorporated a new rule to go along with that, which says "In life your responsibility is to help all others by choosing a service or work that you will enjoy and do this from time to time as it may be needed to help all others in your local community and the world. You can always change what you do by simply going to school and learning something new anytime you want throughout life. Many of us have several hats we wear at different times to be of service to everyone else. For example during the summer vacation I help out at the farm packing house putting labels on packaging and seeing to sanitary measures for food packaging as well as some order processing.

I have a friend that did sewing in the Stetman clothes factory for three years and then decided to change services and go test drive cars for the auto factory. Now she travels all around the world testing cars as her service. She loves it, but we don't see each other much. But that is her choice and I honor her for the choices she has made. I personally love to teach and I will most likely do this for some time to come, except for next year. I will be vacationing in the south of Africa to learn the culture and just relax as my mate and I have planned.

We have harmony, peace, and a balanced sense of purpose for the most part in today's society. We still have some who feel it is not their responsibility to help the world as a whole and will not do any service. All in all, things are well rounded in our society.

Many of the ways we live are very close to what the author from the money era wrote about the future. This is a very good reason to use this book as a study guide for that past era.

Let me read a passage to you from this book on how the author states they would get out of the use of money.

[Ms. Alison continues reading from the book.]
Our current society is so enamored in the use of money, they cannot see straight anymore. They have been battling for centuries against each other over issues caused by using money. The people think that if they fight against each other in courts or on a battlefield, they will be able to get an advantage over others in some way and have more money or maybe bring some peace to the world once they win the battle. All this conflict gives the power of the people over to the system and the system consequently kept growing and growing into the huge, feared-by-all Monster that it has become. History has proved this fighting and warring to be wrong and futile at every attempt. But still they fight, argue, and stress over the issues caused by the use of money without realizing what was causing the arguments in the first place. It is a *money, money, money* society we live in and there seems to be no end in sight, for the people do not realize that it is money itself and what it stands for that causes all the problems. There are some understandings of a higher nature that point to the use of money and show us clearly that this money is the cause of all the troubles in the world. There are many sources among the spiritual groups of the current day known as *channeled entities*. They inform us, *"The only way people in this world will be rid of the governmental control over the people will not be by fighting with it, as this gives it more of your personal power when one fights with it, but rather by taking responsibility for oneself and turning away and ignoring the government and it will crumble."* This is related directly to the use of

money as it pertains to the government control of the era. We must take responsibility for ourselves. The governments are simply manifestations of group consciousness that are based on the way people think as a whole. A change of mind will change one's entire life experience.

The information of this quote is accurate. The people will ignore the government and banks at some time in the future. It is the only way the people will get out from under all that control and chaos of the current money era. Eventually in the distant future, after the publication of this book, the people will finally realize the way out and the word will spread. It is predict that for a time in the somewhat distant future, after people come to the understanding that they are warring on each other because of societal structures (be it religious, monetary or other) that were put in place centuries ago, they will see that money no longer works in the current phase of human evolution. It is hoped that this book will help facilitate this new understanding.

Non-force will bring far greater positive results than force has ever brought. Society will be surprised at what good comes back when you do not force. People will respond in a far more positive manner than if you force your will upon them. No force is a greater force than the strongest pushing force. Turning away from the government and banks is a non-force action and that will bring about the end of this oppression era of money.

The government and banks will fight and try to counteract this when it occurs, but the people will prevail and continue to ignore them. These institutions will fall apart very quickly. Some signs of this can be seen in the present day where many people are eliminating their debts with the banking system through a process called *discharging debts*. They are also discharging tax bills and payments to many other types of debts. These are the first steps in the direction of the understanding that will enable all people to walk away and build a better society that will be far less stressful without money.

The future will not have the harsh controlling courts like we have today. Instead, there will be mediation services developed for the people to use when a dispute between two people arises. There will not be the persecution by the government or the system against the people any more. Humans are not perfect (not even in the future), so there will still be a need for resolution of sorts, but it will not be the harsh control and force that has been used in the past. People will learn to honor each other, which will bring a great deal of honesty and respect to everyday interactions with each other. Because people will honor another's choices, they then will not try to fight, change, control or sway each other from the path of understandings that one has chosen for oneself.

If a business brings a dishonor to a person or a group, a system of recourse will be used instead of fighting in a court. That system will be a global communications system that will be similar to the Internet of today, but far more advanced. All people will be able to post a complaint against or a compliment for any business. This type of system will enable all others to quickly check a score on any business, or, if desired, read the compliment or complaint itself about the business. In this way, a business can judge itself to see if it is providing a desirable service or product for society. Under this system businesses will be far more compassionate and caring toward the people as a whole. They will not make things that people do not want or need. There will be new products that were previously oppressed that are good for the world and the environment and desired by the public at large. There will be no incentive (money) to deceive others like the days of old when money was used. Business will not force products through lies just to sell a product for money that really is of no value to the user.

This new global information system will either kill or enhance a business. Since there is no money to be earned by the business of the new era, there will be no reason for any business to make to old false claims about their products to try to sell them to the people. Many new businesses will be started because they will cost nothing to start and nothing to run. They will be started because the initiators have something they believe is of value and/or of service to the public.

Real estate—yes, this will also be free. All one has to do is check with the local real estate agents for what house or business facility is empty and available and then put his or her name on the list as the new occupant of that building. One may also build a new building on any piece of land that is not reserved by another person. To do this, one will list his or her name on the real estate list as the new occupant and then find a person skilled in construction to build the desired structure. The trucks at the request of the builder will bring in the materials and the building will be constructed while observing safety measures for the new occupants.

[Ms. Alison stops reading and continues addressing the class.]

Class, you can understand from the passage I just read to you that the writer was not too far off in his interpretation of our current society.
Class, I have a small quiz I want you to take on the first part of this book.

Test

Ultimately there is one reason for the way things were in this era. Please answer each question according to what we have gone over so far. The question can be far-reaching and complex but for this test most all reasons can be reduced to the use of money.

Question:	Answer:
1. What ultimate reason would a person want to kill another person?	MONEY
2. What caused oppression?	
3. Why did people of this time have a great deal of stress in their lives?	
4. Why did they try to oppress others?	
5. Explain the downfall of this society?	
6. What did they war over?	CONTROL
7. What was war good for?	
8. What was the source of stress?	
9. What held the people back from freely evolving naturally?	
10. Why do you think the author that lived back then wrote this book?	

Ms. Alison:
Sara, let me see your test. Sara, you have got all but one right here.

I have added one question in here that is not covered in the lessons so far to throw you off. Question number six is the off question. And the answer to all the questions is *money* except number six. That answer is *control*; however, they used money to do the controlling. So there really is no wrong answer if you answered money to this question. I want to continue now with the next section in the book.

[Ms. Alison continues reading for the class.]
Wars
There were different kinds of wars. The wars of the past were mostly fought due to money and control. In times past some wars were fought for land and conquest, i.e. *control*. Conquering others was a means to acquire land and the land had value, so it still was over what we would call *money*. Another kind of war was the religious wars. These wars were a hodgepodge of control, conquest, and money. The main difference was that the religious wars were fought in the name of GOD. I really do not think God ever came to anyone and told him or her to fight a war for Him or in His Name or anything even similar. Do you think God would have done this? Maybe He finds this all rather sporting to watch us down here fighting with each other while He sits back in His lazy boy chair with a beer and chips, betting on who will win. I think not. These wars were all about control of the world by the powerful few and they were all at the minds desire and hand of man.

Many wars have been fought because the government considered them to be good for the economy. You see they needed to build guns, bombs, and warring apparatuses to war with, which created jobs. These wars also eliminated people that the governments felt were expendable, thus thinning out the populations of other countries. It also was used to acquire or should we say conquer other countries for their land. Land has value. Wars were also used to divert attention away from what was really going on behind the up front facade of the government. They would tell the citizens that protecting their country would be good for the people, but war propaganda was really a distraction from the real reasons the wars were generated. A war was a good way to create and place into law a new forms of control, the people would agree easily because the war or issues at hand made the new laws seem a good idea at the time it was put onto the people because it was always touted as being a needed protection for the people from their enemies. They would then vote it in only to find out later that it was not good for them at all and the hidden agenda allowed the government to encroach on the freedoms of the people that much further. This is the small steps mentioned earlier. These wars directed the masses to be more concerned with getting their soldiers home alive instead of questioning the ways of the government. The governments would use wars to create and implement many new laws that suppressed the masses even more. The creation of these new laws provided a means for further and further control and imposing of new taxation of the people within the country of the same government. The further control and taxation enabled the government to create even more wars. One such outfit that was used to create wars was the Central Intelligence Agency (CIA), though there was no intelligence within this agency or in what it did. However, in the latter part of this era, this warring did not work as it had in decade's prior. The people were changing and evolving in consciousness and killing was becoming something the people would no longer tolerate--even killing of the enemy was in bad taste.

Tags

Because of money, all sorts of things were tagged to the people of the money era: birth certificates, driver's licenses, social security numbers, credit reports, criminal records and so on. These are all *tags* and they are all due to the use of money. Jails in this era were big businesses that were run mostly by large private corporations. This was a profitable business because the government pays large sums of money to the operators of these jails to keep large numbers of people locked up. This money came from taxation of the people.

Chapter Two

How Things Were Done & The Reality of That Time Era

[Ms. Alison stops reading from the book to address the class.]

Teddy would you read the first part of "Chapter Two" down to *Controlling the People* to the class?

Teddy:
Yes, Ms. Alison.

The System

First, we consider the minds of the people as they experience the monster the government became. It was so big and instilled so much fear in the people that they would neither act against nor walk away from it because of this fear. It is with good reason that they feared it so much, because the monster had so many brainwashed hired guns to force the people into submitting to their controlling agendas. Even the people that were the enforcers were afraid of the system, which led them to continue enforcing the system's laws even though they may have disagreed with them completely. This was a perpetuation of the problems.

The era of money became harder and harder for all people as time went on. This writing deals only with the later part that, the author, lived in. At this time the USA was about 200 years old and going strong as the world's leading power. But other forces were closing in on it as a new world government was forming. Countries were merging and the United Nations was created. This was perceived by the general population as a bad thing, and it was with very good reason. The new alliances and laws that were created from this meant even more corruption and total control of the people. It meant less privacy and more cost to the people and, of course, more stressful financial burdens overall. We the people are made to pay for the ignorance and stupidity of the government. If one tries to uncover the truth about systemic fraud, that person is labeled a terrorist and is ridiculed; persecuted and locked up for fear that the truth will be revealed to the masses. There is just one way out of this whole mess and that is for the majority of the populace to just walk away from and ignore the system totally. I will say this again: *fighting it will make it stronger and you will not win*. The fear of the government needs to be overcome by the people and once this happens and the people ignore the system, both the fear and the government will subside and disappear all together. Throughout this text you will see a legal distinction in the spelling of the United States and united States, this is accurate for the actual meaning and for the differences between the incorporated and the prior unincorporated type of united States. The lower case united States is the original before the bankruptcy took place.

Going back to the biggest deception before this world alliance was formed, just before the 1930's, when a group of bankers met and reviewed a plan that was devised to take over the united States and bring it under the control of the world banks. The banking systems had been fooling the people of the rest of the world for centuries before this. These bankers were from all over the country–some were originally from other countries, but now they owned banks in the USA. They conceived and executed a plan that would fool the government into accepting it without knowing what it meant. The government passed it into law late one Christmas Eve. The story of this may still be available in some future archives. It is currently available in an audio format known as *The Creature from Jekyll Island*, which we can locate on the Internet. Jekyll Island is located off the coast of Georgia. When the honest politicians discovered this plan it was too late. The money the dishonest politicians received from allowing this plan to continue had already corrupted them and the new system of deceit was well under way. One banker said, "Give me control of a nation's money, and I care not what laws you make."

This plan worked so well that in the current society there is no actual money in circulation. The bankers that forced this plan on the government, and now with the help of the government legal system in the 1920's and 1930's took our real money away from us. They replaced it with new paper notes (Federal Reserve Notes) that look similar to money, but have no real value. President Roosevelt did this when he recalled all gold from circulation. This by the way was done before World War II.

This bank plan also created the IRS, which is known as the most feared government agency of the time. However, this agency was not even a part of the government, but the government would do nothing about it because of its corruption and the enormous amounts of money this agency collected from the people. That money went to the banks to pay the interest on the national deficit the government and banks had created out of thin air. The politicians ignored the illegal taxation because they were elected into office by the large amounts of money supplied to them from the banks. Much of this money was disguised as corporate donations. The banks could afford to buy all the politicians they wanted and they did just that. This corruption would further enslave and impoverish the masses because politicians will not bite the hand that fed them. Passing this law that the bankers imposed upon the government in their rather clever well-conceived way as mentioned is what created the all feared IRS. The fact that this agency was not a government agency was kept secret by both the banks and the government because they knew it was fraudulent. The corruption went all the way to the top of government. Before this plan went into effect, money was considered to be backed by precious metals and a bank had to honor the deposits of its customers in gold or silver if a customer demanded their money in that form. After this plan went into action, all the gold and silver was removed from circulation. Of course this removal was accomplished illegally.

The government did not have the power to take the gold and silver away from the people, but the government told the people that they had the authority to do it anyway. The government does not follow its own rules; they make it up or lie and ignore the rules as they go along. Later a congressional finding stated that president Roosevelt had no such authority to recall all the gold in the country.

Under the new banker's plans, what was to be the backing for the money? It would be the labor of the people. In other words they created paper money out of thin air. There was not enough gold and silver to back up all the money they would create. But there was a great deal of wealth if they would pledge humans as collateral for their deception. They had no authority to do this, as no one has the authority to do something like this without the permission of the people, but of course they never asked or disclosed this to anyone. They just went ahead and fraudulently did it in secret. This created a business corporation out of every child that was born by requiring the use of a birth certificate in all hospitals. These birth certificates did not exist prior to 1933. A birth certificate is simply a contract with the government that is created in fraud and secrecy. This contract just created a fictional overlaid corporate entity to the living male or female child.

It gets even more corrupt than this. They then viewed each person as dead, because a corporation is a fictional entity that needs someone else to speak, act, and perform for it. A corporation cannot do or make a decision for itself, as it is fiction. The federal government loved this plan because it gave them total control over every person in the country that they did not have control over prior to this plan. It was all deception and fraud on their part but they ignored any complaints about it. They also wrote laws that made them immune to lawsuits against the government–how convenient that was for them to protect themselves from being sued or answer for their crimes against the people! The creation of fictional humans needed a system of governance so statutory, and civil law was created. All of this brought every human with a birth certificate into the federal government and under the control of corporate law. This is how the people lost their Sovereignty. This is what has enslaved every man and woman in this Country. Before this, all humans were sovereign and the federal government had no control over the human man or woman. The roll of the federal government had previously been limited to defending the shores of the country and protecting American Citizens traveling abroad, but now it controlled everyone from a Federal standpoint instead of the from state one lived in.

The government controlled everything from food production to television to schooling to the religions of the time. They would no longer allow a choice of religion in the schools. Schools were told what they could and could not teach because they did not want the schools teaching the masses anything that would undermine the government control. One was not allowed to teach his or her children how to live a decent life in any school, but only to fear the laws and to obey them dutifully. The government supported the many police shows that were on television, most likely in the form of tax breaks or kickbacks at a very high level to those that owned the media. As an example to the public, these shows taught the viewers that if they did not obey as instructed, they would never be able to escape the long arm of the law. The law would always find and punish those who disobeyed. This was, of course, an intended message to instill fear in the viewers.

There were many police shows that were all fiction, but they sent a very real message to those who watched them for any period of time: the system is unbeatable, so don't try to usurp it, or the police will find you. This is another stepping-stone of mind control, which has led to the process of writing of this book because it is time we moved on up the ladder of evolution and out of this kind of thinking. Don't you agree?

Taxes were a very deep subject with all people of this era. The people were so afraid of the government that most would not question the forms they gave out each year to collect the illegal taxes they extorted from the people. This was also a part of the 1933 deception as mentioned earlier about the creation of the IRS. Since a person was now a corporation, he/she was no longer a living breathing human or a sovereign in the eyes of the government they could tax you any way they wanted. They had the control~or so they said.

To incorporate is to enter the realm of the government and give them permission to tax your company and tell you what and how to do your business. To the government you as a living man were a corporation. The people also believed that incorporating their business was a good thing because the government said so. People are very uneducated when it comes to law because the government wants the masses to be compliant and ignorant in order to easily control them.

But some did question authority, investigated the real truth for many years, and discovered the truth about the deceptions. Some of these people were punished by being put in jail, which sent a message to the general public to obey or else Uncle Sam would come after them too.
Taxes were a rampant part of existence. There was tax on everything: labor in the form of income taxes, food, clothing, fuel, the roads, in fact there was a tax on everything you could spend money on in some fashion or another. This so called money was only worth the paper it was printed on. This meant that a one million dollar bill in reality was only worth two cents, because that is how much it cost to make it. Because the gold was now gone, this bill was actually worth nothing.

All of this is a mute point, but it bears mentioning. The real point here is that the people were unnecessarily burdened and stressed by a system that did not care for its people or what was done to them. They only cared for themselves and what they could take from the masses of people. The system itself came with a highly publicized saying, "It's not a perfect system, but it's the only one we have." This saying was a cop-out and a way of saying, "Don't bother us, we don't care. Just take what we dish out and go away." As long as you paid them, they would leave you somewhat alone; but in many cases when they found you were a payer of money, they would harass, falsely charge, and threaten you with loss of freedom to get you to pay even more. This was the way of the courts. And they made billions of dollars doing this to the people and most of it was for nothing. I have to say also that there were at times some good things that came from the courts. Some resolutions they came up with were good and did help some people. For the most part it was difficult, costly, time consuming and a lot of red tape that went along with the high cost of hiring an attorney. Many times it would take years to resolve a simple conflict.

This system existed for a very long time. The sad part is that they did not realize what they were really doing. They would oppress the people then punish them for rebelling, when in fact the government started the rebellion by using force and oppression on the people in the first place, long before the rebellion ever came into being. The government and the strong were really inflicting this pain onto themselves by their very own actions upon the people. The people would not have rebelled if the strong or government never oppressed the people in the first place.

The American system of government which, is actually a part of England, is all run in the USA as if it was just an extension of English law transferred to the USA but the system of law still answers to the English parliament for their instructions on how to run the system here in this country. The United States legal system is operated under the laws and control of the British Crown. The people of the united States are considered to be subjects of the British Crown. HOW DOES THAT MAKE YOU FEEL AFTER ALL THE BLOOD WE SHED FOR OUR FREEDOM. This developed by the banks forcing the united States into bankruptcy. The united States was forced to file bankruptcy in England, which is where we adopted most of our laws. This is all done under the guise of the US Constitution that the system just ignores all the time. That is because there are two different Constitutions, the original, and the corporate version. The corporate version is the one they use against the citizens. Please not the small "c" in citizen, it is a legal misleading of the word. This abuse from the system against the people will eventually scar enough people so that they will rise up again against this monster and will want to fight the system. This would be just as big of a disaster as it has always been in all our prior history of wars. Why you say? It is because they may admit defeat again like before but then just come right back into power again the next day, week or year. They will creep back in by the use of contracts and money.

As I have pointed out throughout this book, there is still only one way out of this repeat of history again and again. That way is to turn away, ignore the system monster, and dissolve it permanently by taking the teeth out of the monster all together. These teeth are MONEY. Stop using it and everything will eventually revert back to what it was meant to be by the all that is, our creator GOD. Even to revert back to the original Constitution would be a great stride forward for the sanity of humanity.

In this era this cycle went round and round like a dog chasing his own tail. Those in government did not realize they were the actual creators of the rebellions by the creation of oppression, money, and laws that they inflicted on the people. Many people employed by the system actually thought they were really doing someone some good by perpetuating control and oppression. This was another case of not seeing the whole picture as it was really being played out. Most of these government people did not care at all for the people who were forced to come to them by the demands of the government. They would treat them with disdain and a careless attitude and ignore them and their needs, even though the government people were in those jobs to help the people who were forced to come to them in the first place by the government they were employed by.

Force. The main themes of this money era were force and control. Ironically, non-force is a far greater force than force. Non-force will bring greater and swifter results than force can ever bring, especially in the context of this book. It is surprising what good comes from not using force. People respond in a far more positive way to non-force than if they are coerced. Turning away from government is a non-force.

The systems of governance are creating fear by making laws, hiring people, and brainwashing them to use force against their own brothers and sisters all over the planet. These brothers and sisters are souls just like them. One phrase they use is, "you have committed a crime against the people of such and such city and county." If you are in court for traffic violations (for example, speeding), where are the people you have injured by this speeding? Was there an accident from your careless driving and were there injuries? If not, what is the crime you committed against these people? Where are these people? You should ask the court to produce the persons that have been injured or wronged so you can see for yourself what harm you have done. Remember, a crime is a premeditated action. Everything else is a reaction to a stimulus or action in your direction. They will likely get mad at you if you ask this question. The courtrooms are designed purposefully to intimidate all who stand in front of the bench. This is a fear tactic to get you to do as they say and to believe they are all-powerful. We as people are really very smart psychologically in the way we have evolved and created things like a courtroom that can intimidate most anyone. However, if you know this intimidation factor is at play and you understand it well enough, you will overcome this fact and most likely not even be involved with dealing with such a situation.

Government relies on the people being ignorant and perpetuates this ignorance by limiting funds to schools. They also keep making so many laws that the average educated person in this system would need years of education to understand them if one was to question authority. Ignorance is considered by some people to be blissful; however in reality this same ignorance is killing people. By being or staying ignorant, people allow others to run all over them while others rob them blind and keep them in the poorhouse. In this way the majority of people will not learn what the government is really up to. With most of one's time spent making a living, a person does not have the time or legal knowledge to question the workings of the government. If you are alive in the world of the money era and living with any kind of laws, you are living in a prison—a prison of laws. There is no real freedom under this situation. There is a law for everything you can imagine and if something new comes along, such as the Internet, then a law comes right behind you and say's, "Hey, you can't do this or that because we the system say so," they make another new law to control that too. It is agreeable that some of the laws were good, but only for some purposes, because many people have a lower understanding of life's purpose and are highly pressured to attain money. As such, the systems are well trained in the art of deception and greed due to the use of money. These people cause a major nuisance in other's lives.

When the time comes where the people can't or won't take any more laws, and the entire total control that the money hungry, greedy, power hungry system has lain upon an already over-burdened and highly controlled society will no longer be tolerated. They will likely think that demanding reform of the government is the way to affect positive change in the system. A limited amount of demanding is already under way at the time this book is being written. It is being met with much resistance and frustration. In fact, there are plans within the system to train National Guard personnel to go house to house and round up people that they feel are protesters and non-conformists. They will label them terrorists and imprison them for stirring up the public with the facts and deceptions of the system. The current demands of the people are met with total resistance, denial, and force or the system just ignores the people and there own laws. Demanding will not work on this monster. As I have mentioned before, the only way for the people to take control and change the system is for mass amounts of the country and world populations to just ignore the system all together. Stop paying the banks and the taxman and ignore the legal system all together. Just turn away.

At first the government will try to force obedience of their laws to some degree. When this does not work they will go one of two ways: they will either declare marshal law or they will take sides against the banking system. Most likely they will choose marshal law first but they will find this too will not work. Then they will change spots or change sides and blame the banks for our lot in life. They will conveniently release the mysteriously found truth that they will say they have just uncovered about the fraud of the banking system. They will likely admit that they too were duped by this fraud all along. This also will not work on the people of this future time. The reason this will not work is that the current and the next two to three generations of new souls (people) are far different in their internal mental makeup. The way they will think will boggle the old mentalities. They will recognize lies and deceit very easily and will not tolerate it at all. Some of the new generation souls will be in high places in the system during this time period and they will work toward tearing down and reorganizing the system. No one will ever suspect these new souls within the system. At the time of writing this book there is a law on the books known as the NESARA act. This is a national reform law that will restructure to government and close the IRS and the Federal Reserve banks. Most likely this will be reserved for a last resort effort to keep control of the nation.

Most people don't realize it, but the people have always had ultimate control. They merely feared using it against such a huge monster. Remember the story about Goliath and how easily the stone brought him down; ignoring the system will have the same effect.

Ms. Alison:
Thank you, Teddy. Before we review I would like to read this whole chapter. Oliver, would you pick up where Teddy left off?

Oliver:
Yes, Ms. Alison

Part Two Banks
Controlling People

What happens when a free soul is moved from a free system to a money system? Here are only some of the examples of what happens when a person buys a house, gets married, buys a car, or has children in a money system. This moves one's mentality from being who they were as a child, free and without obligations, into a money controlling mentality of responsibility. This responsibility mode ties one to a job in order to make money one now needs just to give it away to others to sustain one's own life and new responsibility. It's a vicious cycle and a major burden that one takes on for many reasons, be it peer pressure, upbringing mentality, personal beliefs, or beliefs of one's mate, friends and family, etc. But this turns a free soul away from being free and happy to being burdened and chained to money. Most people of this era are not able to see the world and or live a fruitful life especially as a young person.

Instead money creates the mentality that thinks, *I must work hard all my life and pay my bills dutifully so I can retire with a nest egg. Then when I am old and unable to enjoy the world as much as I could have when I was young, I will be able to travel and see a small portion of it before I die.* The amount of travel is still directly restricted to the size of one's nest egg. One is always under the control and restrictions of money.

One may travel the world for work as many pilots do. This is considered to be a great job for most, but pilots are still restricted and controlled by money and from the control of their boss that are also controlled by money. All things in this society are controlled by money. No one is free of this burden, not even the homeless. No one is free of this burden of control.

If one buys a house, one has accepted all that comes with the requirements of earning and paying for that house. In the case of a house, the control and the burden can last thirty plus years of enslavement to money. Now here is a really odd part of the money game and all this control. If one buys a house, one usually gets a loan from a bank to buy the house. But under the current laws and banking system of the USA, the house just purchased is being given to that bank for free, simply by signing a promissory note with that bank.

What this means is under the laws of commerce today, you just enslaved yourself to a bank that did not give you anything at all and got control of your house for free. It only cost them the price of the paper the promissory note was printed on to take your house away from you. You are now a slave to a job and to the bank to pay that amount plus interest and insurance for the house you gave them for free. This all stems from laws put in place, which you are most likely unaware of. These laws have rendered you a slave to the system. These laws are far too long and complex to be listed here. You can find a great deal of information on the Internet under loan and debt elimination services, but remember fighting with the system is feeding the monster. The biggest monsters are the controllers of the money, i.e. BANKS. The banks at the very top of the ladder and are the guilty parties. The Federal Reserve is a private corporation that is in no way a part of the government. However, it does control the government as it controls all other things. It may be good for you to find and listen to *The Creature from Jekyll Island*.

Slaves

You think you are free, but are YOU really.
In reality you are not. You are a slave first to money, which makes you a slave to the banks. Then you are a slave to the job you have for the money that you have to give to the banks. Then you are a slave to the government for the money demanded from you by the government and the control placed upon you through the use of money. YOU have to pay money for everything in life, which ultimately comes from and goes right back to the banks. It's not yours it's theirs. They control the money and as long as YOU are using it, they control YOU.

As most people do we all think all these dislikes we have with the system, then we try to apply our concerns, questions and dislikes upon the system looking for redress and reform to the bad situations that have come about from the corruption of the system. We point these things out to our politicians, judges, police etc. but the problems persist and in most cases continue to only get worse as we do this. It's time to wake up to the fact that they don't care about us or how bad things are in our world. They only thing they care about is your money, controlling you and taking whatever they wish from you.

Taking these matters of legal and societal concerns up with the system is simply a waist of time. Very little change ever comes from this approach. The real changes will only come when we turn away and just ignore the rantings of this monster of a system that we as humans built in the first place, set into motion then let it get out of hand. We need to turn around and treat the system with the same distain, ignorance, and carelessness they are currently treating us with. Ignorance, incompetence and a constant breaking of the laws they have sworn an oath to uphold and treat us with is their way.

Money what good is it?

So I ask, are YOU really free? You slave all your life for money just to give it to someone else to maintain a small spot on earth to park your car, hang your clothes, pay a mortgage on a piece of property you call home, but then you spend over three-quarters of your time at your job just to pay the money you get from the job to others so they will allow you to keep that property, car, furniture and clothes. If you do not pay, someone will come and take it all away from YOU. In the end when you die, it all goes back to the banks and government.

Money is energy. What power does money have? Money itself inherently has no power whatsoever. All the power money has comes from humans placing their power into money by believing money can do things or control other humans. When we believe in money and what power we have placed in it, and then it has power over us.

We are the ones that actually have all the power. We have just transferred or delegated that power to a belief system called money. Take your power back and you are taking control of your life back. No longer can greedy power hungry humans manipulate you through the use of money.

Money what good is it?

On the next page is a two page public document that can be found on the Internet of the money era easily. This document was written by a congressman that uncovered the fraud, deception and control of the banking systems, not just in the USA, but worldwide.

The Bankers Manifesto of 1892

Revealed by US Congressman Charles A. Lindbergh, SR from Minnesota before the US Congress sometime during his term of office between the years of 1907 and 1917 to warn the citizens. "We (bankers) must proceed with caution and guard every move made, for the lower order of people are already showing signs of restless commotion. Prudence will therefore show a policy of apparently yielding to the popular will until our plans are so far consummated that we can declare our designs without fear of any organized resistance. The Farmers Alliance and Knights of Labor organizations in the United States should be carefully watched by our trusted men, and we must take immediate steps to control these organizations in our interest or disrupt them. At the coming Omaha Convention to be held July 4th (1892), our men must attend and direct its movement, or else there will be set on foot such antagonism to our designs as may require force to overcome. This at the present time would be premature. We are not yet ready for such a crisis. Capital must protect itself in every possible manner through combination (conspiracy) and legislation. The courts must be called to our aid, debts must be collected, bonds, and mortgages foreclosed as rapidly as possible. When through the process of the law, the common people have lost their homes; they will be more tractable and easily governed through the influence of the strong arm of the government applied to a central power of imperial wealth under the control of the leading financiers. People without homes will not quarrel with their leaders.

History repeats itself in regular cycles. This truth is well known among our principal men who are engaged in forming an imperialism of the world. While they are doing this, the people must be kept in a state of political antagonism. The question of tariff reform must be urged through the organization known as the Democratic Party, and the question of protection with the reciprocity must be forced to view through the Republican Party. By thus dividing voters, we can get them to expand their energies in fighting over questions of no importance to us, except as teachers to the common herd. Thus, by discrete action, we can secure all that has been so generously planned and successfully accomplished."

End page one public document.
Authors note: The history cycle mentioned above is what the new people that are here now and those coming in now and in the future will be breaking free of.

Two Faces Of A Loan Transaction
The Transaction between YOU and the Alleged "LENDER".
You apply to a Bank or Mortgage Company for a loan to buy or refinance a house or piece of property. They cannot loan you their own assets, other depositor's funds, or their own credit. They need your signed application and Promissory Note. The bank or mortgage company you applied to, is known as the "lender". If the loan is to be secured by real property the lender is also known as the "originator" of the mortgage that secures the loan. The bank or mortgage company either sells or hypothecates your Note before you sign the final papers relative to the loan. In essence they are receiving the proceeds of the sale or hypothecation of your Note before they purchase or accept your note as a "loan to themselves". The bank or mortgage company risked none of their own assets in the so-called loan to you. Rather, they used your note to pay the seller, used your note to raise an asset to themselves, and used the face value of your note as something called "principle" which they say they loaned you and against which they charge interest. Consideration on the part of the lender is non-existent and the note was obtained by FRAUD.

The Transaction Between Your Lender and the Bank
So, the Bank or Mortgage Company, after getting your signed application and Note then applies to another institutional lender (bank) for a loan in exchange for your note. The institutional lender will acquire a security interest in the note the bank or mortgage company obtained from you, on the promise of the exchange for a loan. To perfect that security interest, they must either take constructive possession of the note or file a UCC-1 Financing Statement to give notice to other creditors that there is a security interest being held against the note. The security interest may also reach to the mortgage. The institutional lender may contract with the originator of the note to be the servicer of the note and transfer the note to a mortgage pool to be used as collateral to underwrite the solicitation of investors in mortgage-backed securities. The bank or mortgage company, the debtor in their transaction with the institutional lender and you are the lender in your transaction with the bank or mortgage company. The institutional lender cannot perfect a security interest in an underlying transaction that was absent consideration and was a FRAUD. Consideration is essential to an enforceable contract, and to the perfection of a Security Interest.
End page two public documents.

From the above public document information we can see a planned deception that stems way back into the late 18th century of man's corruption against the rest of the world. As it has been said many times throughout history, *Power corrupts and absolute power corrupts absolutely*. However, this statement does include money in its use of power, but it does not address money directly as the cause of corruption.

When a person has a lot of money, life is easy and sometimes even happy. The unhappy rich people are unhappy because they are constantly fighting to get more money and to keep others from taking what money they have away. On the flip side, when a person needs money but does not have it, life becomes very difficult and hard for that person. The hardships of not having money changes a person from good or pleasant to bad, and sometimes very unpleasant to be around. Many people cover up the difficulties well, but the trouble is still there deep within the mind and soul. If you look closely you will see it.

As sentient beings, humans are already self-governing beings, we need no outside influences to run our daily lives and no outside forces or government to make wars and trouble for our existence on earth. We already instinctively know exactly how to self govern oneself with no help from anyone or any legal body. We must allow ourselves this internal manifestation of our own individual creations to now begin for each one of us and thus it will just be for all mankind.

Ms. Alison:
Thank you, Oliver. Class what did all of you get from the above sections of this chapter? Cathy, would you like to give us your opinion?

Cathy:
Yes, Ms. Alison. I see that there was a great deal of deception and apparent planning for many years for a way to take full control of the entire world. They saw a way via controlling money to be able to control all things and all people completely. It seems that the plans of the banks started long before they actually were able to get it passed into law. I see that there must have been some devious minds at work that for some unknown reason wanted to mess with all things. I also feel that these people did not know what they were

really doing to others or themselves, much less care. I guess this stuff did not affect them so much because they had a lot of money and felt they were in control of it all. It seems they knew the real reasons for what was going on. I also understand that this system was devised during the age of the industrial revolution, but took some time before they actually figured out how to implement it. From today's point of view, we can see that it did not last all that long. It lasted many generations and then the people figured out what was really going on. I believe evolution of the mind and soul can do that—change will overcome any adversity over a period of time.

The creation of control also created a great many things the people had to endure because they did not know what was really happening for so many years. The bankers must also have had to devise and implement this plan of theirs by buying off congress and sneaking it into law around Christmas, because they knew that if the majority of congress had read it beforehand, it would have been rejected. I also see how this plan enslaved the people to money; however, I also see that the people were already enslaved to money before this. I don't think it was as bad before the plan as it was after this plan went into effect. This was because money before the plan was backed by the natural resources, gold, and silver. It was limited in quantity and the banks had less control over the real money. This gave some kind of natural measure to the people, because if the banks did not have resources backing their currency, they could not loan money to people. However, the people were still slaves to the money because of the way currency was backed from the very earliest day of trade—a system that was continually used from generation to generation.

The next thing I see is that the government saw that they could control the people even more with this system in place, so when it was discovered, the government did nothing about it. Government officials must have already been in the pockets of the banks through campaign contributions. I think this is what they called it then, that money was used to get them elected into office. Ms Alison, I really am glad I do not live in that era. I may have lived then, but today is today and we are here now, away from all that heaviness. About gold my mother has a large piece of gold as a paper weight, its really shinny and somewhat heavy. She says she keeps it and rubs it for the health properties that gold has for keeping the body's immune system properly.

Ms. Alison:

Cathy, please, continue with the rest of this chapter. You are doing so well and I am fascinated with your interpretations.

Cathy:
Ok, Ms. Alison.

Next we have the ownership of the people by the system and by the banks because everybody needed money to live. It looks like it was a hand in hand partnership at this time between the banks and the governments. The banks had the upper hand because they controlled the money, but only with the permission of the government to do so. I found it very interesting how they figured out how to get around the original Constitution of the united States by requiring a birth certificate document that was recorded with the federal government as a corporation. I don't know if the banks came up with this concept or the government did. Either way, it was clever and fraudulent, to say the least. But the people did not suspect a thing. They continued living, not knowing anything ever happened. They continued as slaves to the very government they created, trusted, and expected to take care of their protection and advancement in society. However, it all became an awful fraud against the people because a few bad apples made a total mess out of the Constitution. They actually made the original obsolete because the people no longer lived under the original rules. They were instead living under the new rules that were being made, called statutory law, which had nothing to do with the original common laws of the Constitution. I put the common law in because I studied some history on this a few years ago.

I can see how they were able to collect the federal income taxes, because the people were now federal citizens and under the control of the fraudulent system of statutory laws through the creation of the birth certificate. No wonder they could do as they pleased to the people! But what I don't understand here is WHY? What reasons would people have to want to do all this to others? Were they lazy, stupid, ignorant, or just power hungry? Maybe they thought it was good or necessary under that system of money they had. I think it was just for the power that money gave them. The people gave their power away to this system of money and law mostly of their free will for not realizing sooner the effects money had on them.

Ms. Alison:
Yes, Cathy, you just answered your own question. The reason was that money had been so ingrained into their beliefs that they could not see what they were

really doing. We have talked about this before. They actually thought that money was the way. Since they did, they had to make the money system work and they thought they had to make all the people pay for everything the people would need and use in the world due to this mentality of money. There were some very smart people in the world just as there are today. They came up with all these ideas and made them work. The bad thing is that they did not ask the people if they would go along with this plan before doing it. This was the devious part of the minds of the controllers.

Cathy:
I see, Ms. Alison.

Ms. Alison:
Please, what was the next thing you saw here, Cathy?

Cathy:
Well it seems that would be, the smart ones as you mentioned, but not the ones in the system but those that were not corrupt. They were the ones that saw there was something wrong and investigated the issues they saw. They must have been very brave in the face of all the fear caused by the rules that the system was spewing out. But I am glad they did, because we are now better off for it and we did not blow ourselves up back then. I can see how they lived and were made to chase their own tails for eighty or so years in frustration and then they died. The author speaks of the unnecessary burdens the people lived under all because of money, but it was also because of greed and control of those who controlled the money without caring for others.

The people in the system would oppress the rest of the people and think it was good to do that. They must have been really stupid for not seeing what they were really doing to the souls and minds of their own brothers and sisters. I'll bet they thought they were really smart when they succeeded at controlling or knocking others down. They would keep the people in the dark it seems about the actual level of education that was available. A better education would bring a better chance at having a good life even with the money mentality. Today we have a basic living class in the fourth grade that teaches us so many things about our world and how to treat others on all levels. I feel that a very early education in this area sticks with us all our life and makes for a far better, well-rounded person when it comes to treating others fairly and equally. I can see there is a difference in my classmates as opposed to the money era stress that people endured. But the system did not want them to be educated, so with less education and more time spent on earning money they would tend not to ask the important questions of the system regarding *why* things were the way they were.

When the people realized on their own what was going on and started to spread the truth, the government went house to house and rounded them up and silenced them by taking belongings, fining them and putting some in prisons so the rest would not see or here from them. I like the part where he talks about the system that reminds him of a weasel. He says they will fight and then point a finger at the other guy to make themselves look good. Man, I could not ever trust anyone who would do that. They were just as guilty as the first party who came up with this plan, and then they were in bed together on the whole idea. Now suddenly they turn and point a finger at the so-called perpetrator when they were also perpetrators themselves.

I almost skipped over the fraud they committed with the Constitution and the secret bankruptcy. It seems that a great many politicians must have known about this but never let it out to the public. They just went ahead and did it anyway. To me this is one of the most massive deceptions that could have been done, not to mention it was done to the entire country and personally to all of the people. I find myself thinking how the capitalization of one letter in the same word can have a totally different connotation and legal meaning for the word, and I think that their peers should have hanged them all. This angers me so much that I cannot say very much about it.

Ms. Alison:
Ok, Cathy, that was good, but I want someone else to take part two of this chapter. Who will it be? How about you Benjamin?

Benjamin:
Ok, Ms. Alison. From what I remember I can see how this could easily happen to a person—the responsibility thing that is. If I were required to pay money for something, I too would feel just like they did. Only today we do not do that, so we have a different perspective on this stuff than they did. We can easily see how it affected them because we have the perspective of not ever having to use money; they could not because I guess no one ever thought of doing away with money, at least until the author wrote this book. The way I understand it, they did not travel much back then. We can. And I, in particular, have been around the world twice so far. My parents say that it is

best to go see the world while we are young in order to have a better perspective about everything. And we learn so much from traveling around different cultures. It gives us a new way of living our own lives that we would not have chosen before experiencing many different cultures. I believe this makes me a better-rounded person mentally and spiritually. They say we develop a particular perspective when we travel and thus in older years we do not long for what we think we may have missed in our youth. I agree with this because I have been around. I know my aunt has not traveled because she was not interested in traveling for some reason. I think she may have a phobia about going to distant places.

She is a bit different than the rest of our family and it shows that she doesn't seem to have all the experiences and levels of understanding the rest of us have. I can relate to this because before I was ten years old, I had not travel and wondered about a lot of things that I do not wonder about now because I have seen a lot more of other lands and the people that live their.

As far as the slave thing, that has already been covered so with your permission Ms. Alison I will skip this part and go on to the banks.
Ms. Alison:
Ok Benjamin.

Benjamin:
I see how they changed the laws, but it was clever back then for an unsuspecting people to get duped so badly. I don't know where that public document of the bank's manifesto came from, but it sure reveals a portion of the true nature of the fraud they lived with back then. I am like everybody else in this class, wondering *why* they could or would want to do something like this to others. Today we feel what others think and feel by just being near them. I can tell when someone is sick or upset, even if they are trying to hide it. This is because we are so much more open in our hearts and minds which gives us a sixth sense of intuition. It could also be considered a psychic ability they did not so much have. I feel this partly because we do not have all the pressures they had back then. Or maybe it is because we are just more evolved in our consciousness, our feeling center, and our natures, but either way we don't treat others the way they did. We have respect for others and we allow them their choices, like my aunt. No one bothers her for not traveling the world or for her being a little different in her mindset than most. No, we love her just the same. She is all right.

Ms. Alison:
Wow, Benjamin, that was a good way of putting it. Class, we are going to close for the day. Class, I want you to read chapters three and four tonight or in study class for tomorrow's review.

Ron:
Mrs. Alison, do you want us to take notes on this chapter?

Ms. Alison:
No, Ron, just make mental notes so we can go over the facts presented in this chapter for a possible quiz tomorrow. See you all tomorrow.

Chapter Three

Expectations of a new era
Tendencies of the 20th century.

You would think that the world would go into chaos and utter turmoil if we stopped using money. Well, guess what? You would be right and wrong at the same time. You see, there would be at first the tendency for most everyone to go out and hoard food, clothes, cars, fuel and things they always wanted, etc. You would think that everybody would go on permanent vacations and no one would care about anything or anyone. At first, this would be true, especially if we just stopped using money overnight. Even if it were to happen this way, it would not last very long like the chaos that is so often predicted in movies to last for years after some type of world devastation. Remember, the world of people came into existence without money and has survived all this time from the humble beginnings we came from without money. The fact is that people would go a bit wild for a short time, and then they would realize that this is just not going to work at all if they want to survive.

Here is what would happen at first: the chaos mentioned above would be as bad or maybe even worse, however with the use of pre-education via radio, TV, news papers, schools, etc., this would be minimized. Preparation and education of the people is greatly needed for the transformation into the new era of no money. This should be done over a few years' time so everyone could get used to the idea. This could take up to a decade of preparation and education of society.

For the most part people would likely stop buying expensive things during this education period, such as cars and houses. They would want to wait until the plan was implemented before moving into that new home or getting that new car. A stepping type system of eliminating some things that used to cost large sums of money could be implemented during the education phase, like homes and then cars becoming free. The transitions will likely cause cars to be in short supply for a few years until people adjust. I am not saying this will be a smooth transition, but it is a necessary one.

There will still be some that will tend to hoard and go wild in the beginning. The fact of the matter is that the people would come to realize quickly that the chain of commerce they are accustomed to would need to go on similarly to how it operated before they stopped using money. If the new era of no money comes about suddenly by the people standing up one day and ignoring the system, then the pre-education will have to be implemented by the people through TV and radio as an emergency action for teaching the suggested rules and desires for how things should go. Those who instigate ignoring the system long before implementation of the plan begins should develop an education plan, to bring a basic understanding of the self. This is essential to this education. This means that people will have to have a respect for all others and live by that set of understandings. Helping one another will be the priority. Eventually it will help everyone in the overall scheme of things to be fed, clothed, and sheltered at no cost like there was in the past.

Through common sense people will see that if no one grew the food, no one processed the food, or no one delivered the food to the stores, there would be no food for anyone to eat. Many movies of the past predict chaos, looting and even murder over a crumb of food. The people that write these movies have a limited one-track way of thinking. It seems that they are only taking the fear-instilled thinking as their own truth from a government that would wish to continue to control the people. Quite the opposite is far more likely to be the case. Yes, some would go off and live in a cave or in a beachfront house and do nothing, but most would not as they would come to see the need for a service to make sure all things would be made available for everyone and in doing so all things would be available for themselves and the whole of humanity. This same concept would apply to all industries such as housing, transportation, clothing, and so on.

We can already see banding together as a human nature in times of crisis from a disaster. History has proved this time and again. People will come closer and unite in a common cause when it serves the whole. In this case to see that one got fed adequately, one must see to feeding the whole adequately, and thus uniting for the good of all. A basic education of this is essential to make the transition smoother. However, the system will not support this unless the people just stand up one day and turn away from the system. This would force the system to take notice and change for the better or disappear.

Psychological effects

The effects of money and higher pricing were a source of tension. Take, for example, the cost of fuel. The people that controlled the pricing were smart in one sense but very stupid in another. They would raise the price to a very high level for a while until the people got used to the high prices, then they would reduce the price down to the new level that they wanted it to stay at. This was done so the people would feel better about the prices after they came down a bit. The smart thing here is that the lower of the two prices is what made the new permanent higher prices seem better than the really high price that was set for a given time. In the mean time, while the prices were very high, the gas companies made a lot of money. The new lower price is still in most cases approximately double what it was before the price increase. The really stupid part of this is that they did not realize what they were actually doing in the long run. However, eventually this turned out to be better for everybody because they were contributing to the end of money all together. By adding the higher burden of paying out more money for gas, they were adding to the overall breaking of the camel's back that much sooner. With the higher gas prices follow higher prices for food, clothing and all other things. Again, this gives rise to and need for these writings.

However, the actual politics and causes for the price of fuel increases that are so prevalent in the 20th century are not for this book. A complete scrapping of this system is in order rather than a detailed dissection of it, no matter how much reform is made to it. The main theme here is a shedding of the old ways of humanity for a far different and far newer way of living one's life. The upside of this added burden of cost, greed and control in all its forms by the system upon the public is that it will bring the people to the point of scrapping the whole system that much sooner. And we will all be far better off for it. The reason for human existence on earth is not to play politics, but to evolve the self and the soul.

Education

I have previously hinted that people of all types would come to see and understand that if they perform a service, no matter how large or small, long term or short, they are contributing to the whole wheel of society. Even the person that runs a machine in a factory that makes a small part that is used in the making of a car seat button is doing his/her part for the whole and will feel good about the foods, cars, home, clothes vacations, etc. taken freely for one's own life and happiness. This person may do this service for a week, a year, or his entire life. This person may decide to take a year's vacation after doing this service for a time. Or this person may decide to move on to another type of service maybe as a hotel manager or something else. Training is always available for anyone at any time to change service of that which they are no longer happy doing. In many cases the businesses will offer on the job training for the new service. There will no longer be any restriction in getting or learning a new job or service like there was in the money era. Most young people will take up training in the schools before entering there chosen service. A main point here is freedom, mobility, and evolution of humanity and the soul.

During the educational years students will be evaluated psychologically on what they are best suited for in life. They will be encouraged to learn or cultivate that service, art, music, ability, or skill. The schools will be better equipped to handle the needs and requirements of recognizing student potentials. Anyone may attend these schools for a reevaluation of skills at any time in life, because as one grows one changes so a reevaluation of skills may reveal a new job suitability that was not thought of or seen in earlier years.

Housing

As for housing all those all those bulldozers can be utilized and level all the slums all around the world. We can do this easily because housing will now be free it will costs nothing to replace a poor dwelling or business building. Urban renewal will be in full swing as a service to everyone. Cities will become alive with newness and many will be far greater than before. This will be done over a long period of time, as we would not want to take too much from our natural resources too fast. In the start we will just level all those old rundown eyesore buildings. The building materials were already free and have always been free. If you think about it, even in the money era we just went to Gaia (one of the names for earth) and took the raw materials we used for building everything we have. Mr. Lumberjack was never asked by Gaia to pay her for the trees he took. No, she just grows the trees and when we take them she grows more trees for Mr. Lumberjack to take in the future again. It is man that creates the requirement for exchange by way of money or the eye for an eye system. Man says, *if I give you something, which did not cost me anything except maybe some time and labor, you should give me far more than I deserve for it.* This is a greed situation of false creating and taking more than is justified in exchange with others.

Science

Science is another area that will expand immensely because one or more people that are good in science research and development will have no more barriers what so ever in setting up a lab or research facility with all the latest technologies for their work. New technologies, new cures, new inventions, new conveniences, and advanced automation will be coming forth at a greater rate than ever before.

All this will be due to the lack of restrictions that were so prevalent in the era of money. Many new things will be developed and come into our reality of everyday life that were suppressed in the old era of money because no one would put up the money to research and develop them, or because these technologies would limit the control other businesses and government would have over the people due to the newer technologies (such as a better energy source that would not generate constant costs paid out by the home owner in the form of energy bills and taxes on that energy). Science has already found an energy source that appears to be a light in the smallest microns of all things. They are and will continue to learn and understand what this energy/light really is. See chapter nine for better details of what this light is.

People

There will be a huge number of people who will flood the new workforce that used to work meaningless jobs in banks, government, stocks, and insurance, etc.. There will be such an excess of people available even though many do take that vacation or retire a little early. There will still be an abundant number of people to fill all the services that are needed to make the wheels turn efficiently. There will be no shortage of costless labor to fill all as needed. It would seem that most will not want to work, but after learning about the need to clothe and feed oneself and to have a better lifestyle, everyone will come around to the new understanding and most all will help as needed. Do not fret; people will always surprise the world as they have always done.

Law

Law was a tool used to control. It was a very complicated system and was not taught in the normal studies of schooling. The people that were educated in the laws could easily control the rest of the population as they saw fit. These laws were put on the population by means of force. They made these laws very hard for the average Joe to comprehend. There were lawyers and many of them. These lawyers would take clients who were accused of a crime or were battling something with either the system or another person or maybe a company. These lawyers charged enormous amounts of money to deal with the problems at hand—and there were many, many problems in this era of money. All because of money and the mentality of the use of this money. Lawyers were considered blood sucking leaches and with good cause too. They would tell their clients that the situation they were in was a grave and dire dilemma and that it was not going to be easy to win or get out of it. They would tell them that they might be facing a jail sentence if they were going up against an accusation from the system. This, of course, instilled fear into the unsuspecting and uneducated people so they would give anything to get the attorney's help out of the situation.

These lawyers and attorneys would do very little for the clients because they really didn't care about the person, only the money they could get from them. You see the system required the lawyer to be a member of the courts in order to practice law. By being a member of the courts, you were then controlled by the courts. As an attorney you were an officer of the court first. The situation went like this: the lawyers got their licenses to practice, and then they were at the mercy of the courts and were required to do as the courts said they should do. Before each court case came to be heard, there was always an exchange of information between lawyers and the court judge. The judge would in a great many cases make a recommendation or comment on which way he or she felt the case should go. This set the situation against one party or the other in the case. In matters pertaining to the system, such as a police officer making the accusation of a traffic ticket, the court always considered the accused to be wrong even though the law stated the accused was innocent until proven guilty. This is another area where the system ignores its own laws. The person accused of such a ticket would almost always get a fine even if the circumstances proved the person to be innocent or unable to have acted in any other fashion which caused the individual to be ticketed.

These lawyers would then collect their fees up front, so their clients wouldn't stiff them later. They would take the money knowing they were not going to do much or that they couldn't do much at all for their clients. At court time the lawyers and the judge generally knew what the outcome was going to be well beforehand, so they just went through the motions for the clients when they got to the courtroom. Thus we have the word LEACH that appropriately describes what lawyers did. Based on the information presented above, when a person is accused by the system and one hires an attorney they are guaranteed to lose in court. Some lawyers did work for their clients these were mostly in business law where someone may be suing a corporation or something similar.

The world is filled with deceptions and lies.
For example, the system says we are innocent until proven guilty, but when

one is accused of something in the legal system, bail money is required in order to stay free of jail.

Justice

What is justice? Plain and simple justice is punishment of another.

We as sleepwalking humans think we have the right to interfere in the free will of other people. When in fact we do not have the right to do that. As I have explained in book one "Once Upon A Time There Was No Money" we all have the same free will but no right to act against another persons free will. So with that understanding where do we think we have the right to create or dish out something called JUSTICE or punishment of another. Since we all have the same free will there is the catch 22 scenarios of having the free will to do as we wish but at the same time that very same free will dictates we have no right to tread upon another's free will. This also helps to explain what happens to us under the higher rules of KARMA when we do interfere in another's free will. For a detailed explanation of Karma see book one mentioned above.

Now, I ask, if one is innocent until proven otherwise, requiring a bail would indicate the exact opposite is far truer than what is portrayed. Requiring a bail would and does fly directly in the face of saying one is innocent until proven guilty. This would under all circumstances mean that it is illegal to require a bail from someone they say is still innocent. Requiring a bail says that they either want to believe or have already decided one is guilty without any evidence to back up the claim they know nothing about in the first place. There is no logic in saying one thing and then requiring one to pay a bail to keep one's freedom if one is innocent until proof is presented. In fact, this is in direct opposition to the manner as stated. People today will swallow just about anything, especially if they fear the source of the information. This is an example of how backward our system and thinking is on earth under the current mentality of men and women in today's money driven societies.

The explanation given for requiring bail is so the accused will not flee and fail to show up for the persecution session in the courts. To this I ask, why do people want to persecute their brothers and sisters in the first place? And for those that do harm out in the world either physical or emotional to others, I ask why do you do this harm? It is all because of money. The individuals are not really at fault for their actions under such an oppressive and controlling society.

Chapter Four

Education & Transformation

Let me delve into the *now* in this next chapter, which was written for the future. The past negative explanations will tend to be longer than the future explanations because the past has so much illusion and deception woven into it.

Future

After the explanations and co-mingling of past events and future ideations, Let's dwell a bit more on the future, making some comparisons to the past and considering the changes and advances for the future that will soon likely be set into motion.

An education campaign will entail a basic knowledge of supply, demand, immediate need, over-usage, one's service to others, our planet's resources and regenerating and reprocessing existing materials. People will be educated about efficient usage and the history of past generations' greed, and about money and its effects on the mental and nervous systems of the body. A well-educated and balanced person will easily see the need to partake in the overall well being of their brothers and sisters, such as shaking a brother's hand instead of punching him in the face as we did in previous times.

Products and food will be a win-win situation for all. Creating these things may be similar to a job as it was/is in the era of money. The personal benefits will far outweigh the old ways of working for money to support oneself. Instead of working for money and buying only what one could afford with the limited amount of money one may have earned based on ones abilities and education levels, one will be able to have all that one needs and or desires with this absence of money. Money, greed, and a lack of respect and honoring others caused this limitation. All were paid differently, so there was a tier of what one could afford in life based on one's earning abilities.

In the new way if you do a service large or small, you can get everything you need and anything you want. We only ask that you take what you need, no more. For example, only take one car or truck per person for the next 2 to 6 years, and then recycle the old car for the raw materials. Only take one house per family to live in, rebuild, as you need to, but not so often as to produce a higher need for new raw materials to be taken from the earth. You can have the toys you want in moderation; if you are tired of a toy, such as a boat, an ATV or clothes, please give them to others to use through the used product stores or take them to the recycling facilities.

You are asked to not hoard and indulge yourself excessively. Always think of others in our world, as they need the same or similar items as you need. Respect and honor all others as equals to yourself and play well together.

There will be a greater demand for supply than before, but this is to be expected for the first generation. After that people will be more settled because the inner need to hoard will lessen as the generations pass. However, the supply may well be limited during this second generation due to people taking many long vacations. This will only heighten the need for people to re-enter the service force to make sure they too are fed well. Long vacations will also create a lack of transportation services at first, but this circumstance will taper off when those who are traveling start to help out as a service to others. This means that those who love to travel will, in many cases, be the ones that do a service in an airport or a travel agency for the time that they are in a given town before traveling to another place.

After this initial adjustment period generation, the new generation of souls will run the system far more efficiently and conservatively. A proper education from a very early age to learn how to live life to the fullest will prevail, as will the overall understanding of the importance of growing and evolving as a person rather than just getting by and existing.

Transportation

There will be many advances in transportation. Cars will change in the way we drive and propulsion will cease to use the internal combustion engine. The roads will have a substance in the lines painted on the roads (or some similar means) that the cars will use to autopilot the car. This will almost eliminate human error and accidents. The cars will be able to be programmed for a destination and the people will be able to sit back and enjoy the ride or sleep if the people prefer to not drive themselves. And, yes, people will need to know how to drive in the event they need to do so at some time. There will still be windows in the cars for enjoying the ride, but they will darken at the touch of a button electronically from mild shade to total black as desired.

Propulsion will be developed in the areas of magnetics, water, and light energies. These areas are not understood at all in the latter era of money.

Antigravity will be developed in connection with magnetics research to aid the type of propulsion used in cars. Science of the current era has not yet tapped the potential of what kind of energy and power is held in a light beam. Magnetics were only used in conjunction with electricity to create a rotating force field to rotate a magnet within a stationary housing. To say the least, it was a limitation for the use of the magnetics of the time. These magnetic motors still required a source of electricity from an outside source. This source came at great cost and was mostly piped great distances to get to the motors. The lighting of the time also used electricity from an outside source and at a cost.

Communications

The future will have a small device that is carried on the wrist or in a pocket that will allow the user to communicate in several ways all over the world and beyond if needed. This device will surf the Internet (as it is called in the 20th century), it will make phone calls, you may watch miniature three dimensional holographic TV on your wrist, store schedules, maps, travel plans etc. It will talk to the user and answer questions through a logic programming, it will remember years of conversations between it and the user for instant retrieval, it will be able to record anything the user ask it to, it can hold more data than is conceived of from past devices (i.e. it can hold five years' worth of constant twenty fours a day video with ease), it can reason an answer from a question, it can learn how the user formulates questions so it can answer poorly phrased questions with the required data, it may be able to display the same miniature holographic 3-D images by project them on a screen for larger viewing, and it is all done via voice activation. It will only be approximately two Inches Square and a half-inch thick.

In the past the most advanced communications were the wireless radio, phones and the Internet. When the Internet came along, it was good for a while. But like all other things in this era, the government intervened and infected the Internet like a virus infects healthy cells. The government dug its way in and started to track everything and everyone. Over time they attached communication protocols to it, taxed its usage and controlled it heavily. In the early stages you could make a free phone call to anywhere in the world at no charge. The people loved this, but it was unfortunately short lived. The government along with greedy businesses moved in and quickly regulated, controlled and ultimately choked the life out of the free phone calls and then went on to choke the rest of the Internet nearly to death. What seemed to be a great form of communication and source of information became a form of tracking of everything from people to money to travel etc.

Tracking

In the future tracking will still be used, but only to find someone if a phone call does not reach them at first and there is suspicion of trouble. Tracking will be done through the communications device. There will no longer be the need to track a person to persecute them in any court or tribunal because those will not exist. The tracking devices will be in the communications devices carried by the person. The person seeking another person will initiate this tracking in the event of suspected trouble. They will simply ask their own communication unit to find the persons unit they are seeking. This will be instantaneous.

In the past they tracked, and spied on everyone through the Internet, satellite, and phone lines. They hired and trained people to do this tracking. Of course this all cost money, but instead of using all the money they had or could create out of thin air, they taxed and further burdened the people with this through communication charges. Remember, human greed to get ahead was factored into this scenario of charges that were made before the government put in for its share of the pie.

As anyone with a phone in this era would agree, they had to pay heavy taxes on communications. This just added insult to the injury of communication charges, which were high enough to start with. In the beginning of the year 2000, an average phone bill could range from $35 to over $500 each and every month just for a home phone. Business phones cost a great deal more than this for a medium- to large-sized company.

Security

The presence of security in the future will lessen as the need diminishes through the availability of free things for everyone. It will also be diminished by the understandings of all peoples on the planet that will want to live in harmony with all others as a one-world people.

In the past it was understandable in the era of bitterness between nations and cultural races that nations wanted to know if someone was planning an attack. Since the Internet was a global communication system, this security was a necessity, especially since there were many threats of terrorism from other countries as well as a country's own citizens.

By now you can likely guess who was responsible for the creation of these attacks. Yes—the system and its oppression of the people. The system would have to extend itself to protect its people because if they permitted them to all get killed in attacks, they would lose a lot of income from the labors and taxes they demanded from the people. Who then would make those nice clothes, build their houses and cars and harvest the food they consumed. In addition there was the possibility of the system perpetrators being killed in an attack, and of course that just would not do. So they would go the distance and police the Internet for signs of terrorist plans of attack. But remember the system was the perpetrator of the problems that caused the terrorist attacks in the first place. It was not the everyday Citizen that went to other countries and provoked the trouble that became a retaliation from one country to another.

The presence of security over the Internet was a good thing because the people that did not create these attacks wanted to feel safe from threats of terrorists. They relied on their government to supply this protection, all the while not realizing who and why the attacks were being initiated against the innocent people in the first place. The government created these attacks upon the average citizens by way of forcing their ways onto other countries, their wars in other countries and by stealing from other countries, etc. They evoked attacks from their own citizens by means of oppression, limitation, and control of the masses to the point that the citizens would sometimes crack under the pressure of the whole mess. Many hundreds of people lost their lives due to citizens attacking the government. What the government did not realize was that they were bringing these attacks upon themselves as well as the rest of the people by their own activities and control. Spying on the Internet also gave rise to paranoia of being watched by the government just to add a little more stress to the lives of the already stressed people.

During this past era of money, there was excessive abuse of the Internet by the people because there were so many demands on them for money. This new Internet created a new avenue to advertise things to sell in very large quantities, which was cost effective at first. Greed changed the cost factor in a very short time. People who shared the money era consciousness abused all sorts of things in life from the Internet to stepping on delicate tundra in the high country parks out of sheer ignorance and under developed sense of purpose, which was of course due to the system and its control. This was all related to the attitude of the era that was generated by greed and rebelliousness that stemmed from the use of money and excessive control by the system. People did not honor others at all because they did not know any better. People were not taught what life was all about. They just knew they had needs for more money because of the demands placed on them from government and businesses just to sustain life. They did what they could to get ahead and to get that money.

Respect

The future is a place of respect for all other forms of life, human and animal as well as plant. The people of the future will understand that the earth sustains their physical bodies and that they should respect the earth for that very reason. When a person is taught from a very early age about life and its creation and why one is in the physical body, one will not abuse others as one grows to adulthood.

In the past everybody at some point in life hated the way things were. They did not understand who they were and why they were on earth, but they tolerated their existence for the most part, thinking that it was necessary and that there was no better way. Instead of changing things, they just continued to live with their ignorance and oppression from their surroundings.

Law

In the future law will not exist—it will be something different. It will be a suggestion, not a mandate. Laws will not be required because people will not try to harm others or take from them against their will.

In the past people would say we needed laws and order. But this is exactly what creates the need for more and more laws. Some people just cannot deal with all the laws there are, others thrive on them. (Hint: lawyers.) We all live on this planet together. The Creator did not put so many different cultures on earth to pit us against each other. Instead the plan is to see what we will do with *free will*. Free will is an interesting idea developed by our Creator. You could say it was a big joke in a sense, but there is a grand plan to see if we will fight or unite.

The system of the past did not care about its people, but proceeded to persecute its people to show the rest of the people that if they did not obey the system, they too would be persecuted and further controlled by the system. This was such a lovely way to live, don't you think?

A free soul will not stand to be controlled for very long. It is not human nature to be caged or controlled. Nor is it in the nature of the evolution of the soul. The soul is not of this world and will never be subject to mentally created restrictions of any kind. Just look at how many wars there have been throughout the era of money. Wars are due to one rejecting the control of others and for the acquisition of greater wealth.

Divine law and free will

To prove free will exists and how it works, Let's use an example. This will be a recent occurrence around the time of writing this book and possibly hard to read for some. Free will is such that no unseen force will ever come in and stop anyone from doing anything one chooses to do, no matter what it is. Can you say you have ever witnessed an unseen force from above coming down and stopping a person from doing something they have chosen to do? An example of this would be the destruction of the twin towers in New York City or the Columbine school shootings in Colorado or any other disaster or war that has transpired in history. No force has ever come in and stopped these tragedies. It was seen and recorded by the *all that is*, but it was not stopped. The reason is *free will* that was setup by the *all that is*, or God as we like to call it, during the creation of this universe. We can do as we please, but our actions have consequences to them and will have to be balanced out before we are allowed to evolve from earth to the higher realms. Man does not have authority to judge or persecute one another. (More on this in a later chapter on evolution.)

The new mindset of the future generations of a non-money era will have an understanding similar to a popular TV show of the time known as Star Trek. In this show they had a Prime Directive of non-interference. In addition to this understanding, there will be additional understandings along the lines of compassion, trust, personal inner growth, truth, evolution and interactive participation with all other humans where one helps all others by his or her participation in the capacity one is capable of without claiming one is doing more than another.

Freedoms

The future will have many more freedoms in all areas of life, from living anywhere in the world to the foods one likes to eat. No one will try to restrict another because they will respect and allow others their choices.

In contrast, in the past there was lack of freedom in many ways even though they called the USA the *Land of Freedom*. There are far too many to go into, so I will only list one small example: freedom of speech. There is a law that says all people have freedom of speech, yet in many cases one is shunned or fined for using this freedom of speech. For example, the courts and churches say you cannot use certain words that exist in the language. To use a word like *fuck* in a church would get you shunned and reprimanded from the pastor and the other members. If you use this word in a courtroom, the judge may charge you with contempt of court and fine you. Here is the irony of this scenario—freedom of speech says you can use any words you like, but yet when used you get hit with a fine or shunned, which by the very nature of the law of freedom of speech would be illegal for the judge or anyone else to do. It is also coercion for the judge to force anything on the person using the word(s) because of the freedom of speech law. I ask you, the reader, where is the logic in this? If one is free to use the words of the language, why then is one not able to do so? Why are the words in the language in the first place? And why do they think that one word is bad and others are good? What form of logic are they using?

If the language contains a set of words, then the people that speak that language should accept all the words of the language as written in their dictionary. If you cannot accept all the words, then you cannot accept any of them and should speak another language.

There is also a big misconception among the people of this era that using the Lord's name in vain is a sin. First, there is no such thing as sin because of free will. This does not need any further explanation except that if there is free will, then there cannot be sin. You cannot do a wrong in the eyes of the Creator in a free will universe as the systems and churches would have you think. It is not acceptable to use these words on the radio or television, so they use the same word from another language to say the same thing, but that is considered okay to do. They will use the word friggin' in place of the word *fuck*. Friggin' means the same thing in another language. We also have the rebellious nature of the children that are taught that some words are bad to say. This only inspires us to use these words more often than we would if no one ever told us that these words were *bad* to use.

Medical

Medicine of the future will be easier and people will get better treatment than a trial and error type of treatment. The future medical technologies will employ magnetics, harmonics, light, sound, and color into the overall healing systems. Doctors will not use radiation or prescribe drugs as a trial and error method of healing. They will analyze the body's harmonics, magnetic balance, and polarity systems' alignment. From this analysis the physician can pinpoint exactly where the error lies and rebalance it with magnetics, light, lasers and medications that will rebalance the entire system, which will permit the body to quickly heal itself. Recoveries from injuries like broken bones will amaze the doctors of today in how fast they will heal and recover. The body that is rebalanced back into its proper state will heal things like cancer automatically. This rebalance will include the mental state of balancing using things like conscious breathing and awareness of one's thoughts. New technologies will be developed in the areas of magnetics and light, color, sound and more. Sound alone is a great healing device as it deals with vibration on many levels and frequencies. Sound will be used to clear the mind and body of stress very quickly and allow rebalancing in its many forms. There will be many other advancements that this writer is unaware of at this time.

In the era of money, the medical community with all its technology was a bit archaic. They used to believe that cutting out diseased tissue was the way to cure the body of illness. They did not understand very well how the body really worked. They knew about, but did not explore, information pertaining to the electromagnetic field of the body that can heal itself when properly put back into magnetic balance and alignment with all the other systems of the body. The body works as a unit when in balance and will run strong without getting diseased until it gets knocked out of balance. The imbalance can come from many sources, such as a person's belief patterns due to programming from upbringing, a trauma, or just general temperament of the person's mental state. It can come from a work condition or a physical injury. In many cases in the past, a disease came from the poor chemical laden foods people ate. The medical community tended to address the physical aspects of a person most, while ignoring the rest of the system that they could not see.

When a patient was diseased they sometimes used radiation to kill off the diseased cells but this was with great cost to the person both in money and in health, because the radiation was also killing the person as well. All disease develops by an imbalance in the whole body. Things like cancer are nothing more than a manifestation in a part of the body due to an imbalance either in that area or some other area—such as the belief patterns of the person. To heal cancer one would first rebalance the whole system and then the cancer would clear up on its own. The body has the ability to even overcome all those chemicals found in the foods of the day. However, some treatments may still be used even in the future on the harder or more advanced manifestations of disease.

Recycling technology

The current and future developments of recycling technologies will be put in high gear as they will be needed in the future, whether there is a money system or not. The necessity for this will be due to higher production of many products and an increase in population size. Metals from all over the country that are sitting in fields, junk yards and back yards will be recalled for making new products. This will be necessary to help slow the mining of new raw materials. Recycling is less devastating on the environment. This goes with the example of keeping a car for a specified time then returning it to a recycling plant for disassembly and reuse of its materials. However, a car also may instead be given to someone just starting to drive. There will be some salvage yards that will keep cars for vintage parts, but there will be fewer of these yards. Most people will likely return the cars for recycling in these future times. The current salvage yards of today will become high tech recyclers of raw materials.

They will strip the cars apart and send the recyclable materials to the appropriate recycling plants. Some will become large enough to become a plant, which melts and reforms the metals, which then will send raw supplies to other manufacturing plants. Some cars will be kept for vintage collections in the decades to follow, the same as we do today. People will still love the old motoring age of cars from the past. As we evolve to higher understanding of the mind and soul we will put less and less emphasis on nostalgic items. We already know these things are temporary and do little for our evolution in the long run.

These recycling plants will be sending raw materials out such as rubber, metals, and fluids of various types and so on. The recycling abilities will greatly help the days ahead, especially in the era of no money. Issues of cost will no longer be a factor in building new technology to recycle most anything that can be recycled. Today, paper, glass, and metal are the only large recycling industries because recycling these is cost effective and profitable to the recyclers. All will better understand a greater awareness of limiting what we take from Gaia. In addition to this, there will be even greater need of raw materials because the world's population is growing all the time.

Many of the technologies for the future are already known today but are considered too costly to make and use. Again this will not be an issue since there will be no money to take into account to build and use these technologies. Only the cost to the environment will be a factor.

Supply and demand

When this new system comes into play, there will be some adjustments to make during the transition period. It is expected that the current population's approach to job-free living will be such that many people adopt the non-working attitude, and go off and relax for a period of time. As I have stated before, this will be a short-lived situation as food and products that they also need and desire will come into short supply. This is when people will come back into the service workforce to re-apply their talents for their own good as well as the good of all others. There will be a new understanding and meaning of the word *work* at this point. Of course, pre-education to this new era is best.

There is such a vast amount of people with many different levels of personal preference in the world that there will always be someone to fill a particular service no matter what type of service may be needed. Since there is no more money, the question of security and trust will fall away as well. After all, under this new non-money system, what is there for a person to steal?

A whole new mentality toward work, products, and helping the rest of humanity will flourish. Many people love to work with their hands and build things, even now. These people will likely be the construction workers of the new era and will be doing it for the love of it, with an attitude of knowing they are a part of the overall new awareness and respect for others. The adjustment period will teach us all the value of doing things we like to do that will help all others. With advanced understanding and new technologies the cheap stuff found on the shelves today will fall away in place of quality products. Robotics technology will also automate many products as well.

The new era will eliminate the accusations that were so prevalent in the old era. Example: Today, people accuse others for not pulling their own weight in some way, be it either money contribution or the amount of contributions of time or labor. This is due to the instilled mentality in the money era and what is considered to be fair using a money mentality of exchange.

In the future after the adjustment period, people will not think this way because there will be no more exchange of money and the mutual respect they will all have for each other. This in itself will cause people to do more than the same person in the money era would do. In the money era there is a tendency to be lazy or to try to get away with something by doing less than others. As foods improve in nutritional quality, the people will be more energetic in nature and will have the desire to help out in any way they can just because they have the energy to do something for the rest of their community. Most people do not like to sit and do nothing for very long. In the money era there is poor food nutrition because others do not care about the health of the population; they only care about how much money they can squeeze from the product (food) that they sell. Under this mentality all kinds of very cheap low quality foods are made and sold that are full of chemicals but not good for the body at all. They use these chemicals because they are cheaper than the real thing; they use rotting foods that are treated with chemicals to make them taste good, but are just not good for the body.

Education

Future education will start at an early age to show the children how to live in harmony with all other people and cultures on earth.

The education system of the past did not teach people the value of good health and what would happen if they ate these chemicals. It did not teach the ways of harmony, only the ways of money and greed at the expense of others. There is much concern that the government is at the root of our poor food quality, lower education levels, and low standards of living. It is believed they control and initiate feeding us poor foods so there will be even more unhealthy people. An unhealthy person will not have the energy to improve himself very well. This also is so people will need medical care far more often, which equates to more medical products being needed, which then creates more taxes on both the labor of the people in these professions and on the medical products.

All this greed and control is a very big detriment to the population. As a whole it is the cause of much non-caring and laziness in the population.

Health

The future will bring people better, healthier bodies that will live far longer than we currently see. Along with better quality foods, the mental state of the body will be faster and stronger and have an overall glow due to the body being cared for as a whole unit of consciousness. When the body is properly balanced and food intake is within moderation it can process anything that is put into it.

In the past the poor quality of food was also the cause of obesity in so many people. One such example was the vast amount of soft drinks consumed every day. This drink tasted good to most, but it was made with carbolic acid, which can eat the paint of your car. In the human body it strips all the vitamins and minerals from the body and damages the cell membranes. This breakdown leads to lethargy and many illnesses. It causes many things to go wrong in the body much earlier than age alone would do. If you stopped drinking this beverage for two months and then drank some again, it would not even taste good to you because the body would have adjusted to the lack of this acid and the tongue would have changed and healed. The food a person eats taste better when the tongue does not have to overcome this acid tearing down the taste buds. This holds true for many of the foods found on the store shelves today, even though each has its own degree of detriment in the body.

Future manufacturers of food will not last if they make foods that tear down the body. Chemicals will not be tolerated as they are today. This will be due to the mentality of non-money and non-greed when it comes to making foods and because the people will be better educated and aware of the things they eat to maintain good health. The old ways of production will be a thing of the past, so why would anybody want to make cheap non-healthy foods? As part of the education for the coming of the non money era it is essential to look at the spiritual and health food sectors of the day for proper training techniques for future food production.

Religion

Religion will become a thing of the past as people start to understand whom they are and why they are on earth. They will see that what was good for the past is no longer good or appropriate for the present. They will move into a state of permission and compassion for all. This will lead them away from rigid religious beliefs.

In the religion(s) of approximately the last 2000 years, the same beliefs have been misinterpreted over and over and continue to be reinterpreted until they have become chaotic. The people of the money era would go to a church and worship an idol on Sundays; while during the rest of the week some of them would go out into the world and do really bad things to the rest of the population. People thought that if they went to church and confessed their so-called sins that they would get into heaven when they died. All I can say to all that is wow! What a misled group of people! The early religions sought to control the people by telling them the only way to get to heaven was through Jesus and the church. They did this so the church could ask for money from the people to stay in business. There were some really good people that believed that the teachings were good (and for a fair part they were good, but only back in the beginning of those teachings).

You see, what was brought through the veil and taught back then was appropriate for that time and maybe the next 500 years, but no further. This is because people evolve and understandings change over time and new ways are needed to keep the evolution of the soul moving on its path as it was meant to be.

As this book is being written, the ones that can see better than the rest may see the masses as a blind misguided pack of cows. We feel a little sorry for them, but we understand that this is their choice and we honor them for their choices. They believe in teachings that are very outdated and will only keep one in servitude to the system or church that they may think is the way to heaven. There are many ways to this heaven, no one way is better than another but the old ways no longer work, besides there is no heaven as portrayed in the religious texts.

As for the separation of the churches and the governments, there was a falling out of sorts and the members of government wanted to kill God so they could try to become God in God's place. This is noticeable in the ways the governments have removed and even made it illegal to practice any kind of religion in the school systems.

The teachings of the early times instructed that God was outside of the person, when in fact; God was and always will be inside the person. There is no need to worship anything outside of oneself. There was a movie called *Stigmata* that portrayed a truth that was taught at the beginning in the year zero which says, "Lift a stone and you will find me, split a piece of wood and I am there." This was taught way back then and is still true today. However, this is not taught in any churches because this tells the people they do not need the church or an idol as a medium between the person and God. It was good for the time it was taught and is still valid today, but has been removed by the church from their current teachings. It is also said in this move that "those who figures out the true meaning of these words will not taste death".

To take this a few steps further, you do not even need to lift that stone or split that wood to find God, or the *all that is*, because God is a pure form of energy that is all around and exists throughout every molecule of everything there is. God is the energy that creates everything and binds all things together. It molds everything into what it is by the use of vibrational frequencies, geometry, and light refraction. Light is also a vibration. Different colors are perceived because they vibrate at different frequencies, thus making them appear to be different colors. The eye and the brain perceive and interpret the vibrations differently, so we have depth and color and 3-dimensional shapes. If everything stopped vibrating, the universe would cease to exist. Water vibrates at a frequency that makes it appear liquid but when you boil it, it vaporizes and becomes a gas lighter than air. If you freeze it, it becomes hard and dense to the touch—all you are doing is changing the vibration of its molecules.

Critics

Naturally, there will be many critics of this material, which is understandable to a degree. After all, the era of money lasted a long time and became a deeply ingrained way of thinking and operating in the world. Under this system one gave one's personal power away to others; the acquiring of power is something many humans seem to like a great deal. This has become ingrained in us as humans over many eons of time due to hoarding and lack in the harsh climates of our early ancestral time on earth. We lacked the tools we have today to feed and clothe ourselves in an abundant way, so fighting over the limited supply of necessities is one of the ways our fighting started in life. The worst complaints will come from the rich and powerful people. They will say this cannot work; they will argue strongly against it. But the very poor that they have taken so much from outnumber the rich by three to one or better. The poor and the struggling middle class will be the ones to usher in the era of *no money*. They will take the power away from those they have given it to and then the rich will be on the same level as the rest.

I was told more than once in this life by a judge or other person(s) in political positions that "this is the only system we have and if you can come up with a better way, please let us know so we can try something new." I guess that phrase stuck with me somehow and now, so many decades later, here we have a better way written of in this book.

While writing this book, I have been informed of a very real scenario that is secretly under way. The government is secretly training most all the National Guard people in the USA on tactics of search and seizure by going from house to house, rounding up system protestors, labeling them terrorists, and taking them to concentration camps. I do not see this happening on any kind of a publicly recognized scale especially in the media but if it does happen, they will be declaring marshal law for this period when they begin this. As stated, they know what and why the problem is and yet they will not correct it because of all the corruption in the system and a lack of desire to try anything new. Mostly I feel it's because they do not believe in the fix or they do not fully understand that the problem at hand is the use of money.

Some of the critics will be analysts and psychologists that actually believe that a non-money system could not work. They will draw their conclusions from the past history of wars, their own limited understanding and visions that are all based on the continued control of people while drawing on their own past experiences of control with money. Some will even base their beliefs on science fiction movies that show devastation of the earth in a future time. However, they would need to let go of the old energy thinking and envision a society that can work in concert with each other and each nation to coexist on the one and only planet we all live on together. I think some of the past wars were fought because the instigators may have thought that they could actually get the people they were conquering to either get off the planet somehow or that they could just wipe them out all-together for reasons of hatred. I am sure there were many different reasons, but they all had stems of control and greed, which of course comes from land or monetary wealth.

Chapter Five

Class review chapter three & four

Ms. Alison:
Good morning, class. How is everyone? Class, well to get started, as you can see from last nights reading assignment, the reality of that period was far different from today. Those people lived under far different circumstances where stress was a daily way of life. We are not perfect today, but we are at least consciously intending to better ourselves by our personal achievements and better our way of life for all rather than just take advantage of others as they did in this era we're now studying.

I trust you all read chapters three and four. That was quite a read, wasn't it? The author put some things into perspective for you, I hope, so you can further understand this time period.

Ron:
Ms. Alison?

Ms. Alison:
Yes, Ron.

Ron:
I have to agree with what Gail said yesterday about being glad she did not live in that era. How could they have lasted so long living that way? Riinngg ....

Ms. Alison:
Who was that?

Sam:
Ms, Alison, it is I, Sam.

Ms. Alison:
Please turn that off, Sam.

Sam:
Well, I can't, Ms, Alison, because I put my communication chip into this old Rolex watch I got from my grandpa and since then I have not been able to turn it off.

77

Ms. Alison:
I would suggest you leave your communications unit at home tomorrow.

Sam:
But, Ms. Alison, I will not be able to call my girlfriend or watch the games at lunch. Plus all my class notes are in here too.

Ms. Alison:
Okay. Then may I suggest you put that chip back in the case it is supposed to be in?
Now class, we will go over this to see what everyone learned about history from these two chapters. I would like you to do a comparison of then and now for each topic included in these chapters. Let's start with the first one in chapter three. Sam, would you like to start today?

Sam:
Yes.
Tendencies of the 20th century.
From reading this section I see that the author knows that it will be hard for the money era people to make the change. I feel that is because they were so accustomed to a long history of the same ways of thinking. We did not have to go through that transition period, so it is a little hard to imagine what that must have been like to go through. Speaking for all of us, I think we all feel very lucky that we do not live under the stress and oppression of what must have been a dark cloud over the entire planet that was ready to pounce on anyone that the government thought was not a conformer. In the beginning he says that there would be some chaos. Did that happen, Ms. Alison?

Ms. Alison:
Yes, Sam, there was an adjustment period as the author mentions. It was a little different and lasted most of the time of the first generation. It seems that the generation that went through this period kept talking about the past when they used money. That kept bringing up the conflicts and questions in the next generation because they wanted to know more about their parent's ways of life before the children were born. However, the first generation did live a far better lifestyle after money was removed. They were also the ones that made the plan work and grow into the lifestyles we live today that are without the stress and chaos of the money era.
Sam, please continue

Sam:
I also agree with us not using money. He said that we came from humble beginnings and that money was not a part of our creation or existence for a long time as we evolved from the caveman days up until man started using money. This is important to mention, I think, because we are born just as the caveman was without money and when we die we leave earth without money. So, why then did they think money was a requirement while on earth? It is hard for me to understand this requirement from our way of life today. I must say I am glad we do not have this way of life.

Ms. Alison:
Thank you, Sam. Let's have Gwen take this next section on psychological effects.

Gwen:
This section talks about product pricing. They used this to control the level and quality of their standard of living. It seems to me that it was a way of keeping the ones that had less money down so they were not able to attain the same levels as the more powerful and rich people of the time. This is not something I or we are used to today. I can see how this led to the discomfort for the people back then. Psychologically, this could and did cause much unrest in a person, because I would imagine the people felt they were just as deserving as the others that had a better way of life, they just may not have understood why they were made to live with less comfort and status than their counterparts.

We do not try to keep others down, why would we do that? We are all the same inside. We are all from the same energy of creation and we are all connected together by that same energy that created the clouds, water, earth, germs, dinosaurs, birds, the desk I am sitting on and everything else. We all feel the separation of body because we have mobility, but on a grander level we are not separate at all. We are even connected via the molecules in the air between us. One such example is that when I speak you can all hear me because of this connection in the air. It is through vibration of the air molecules from my mouth to your ears. There is no separation between us, otherwise you would not hear my words that travel on the blanket of air that is vibrating when I speak—that blanket is a part of your ears too. Distance makes this seem disconnected, but it is not. Vibration diminishes over distance, but the energy does not.

Ms. Alison:
Thank you, Gwen, I like your understanding of us all being one. Who will take the next section, education?

Harry:
I will, Ms. Alison

Ms. Alison:
Thank you, Harry

Harry:
From my understanding of that era, there were different types of education available. Some no longer exist—such as law schools. But to get to the newer understanding the author was referring to, I see that a basic education about humanity and loving and respecting all life was his message. If we disliked others and ourselves we might start warring with each other again. So an education on the finer aspects of knowing who we are, where we came from and why we are on earth in the physical realm is what keeps us from being as barbaric as the past civilizations were. We are able to, as he stated, change services at any time we wish and do something different when it strikes our fancy. We do need to be taught the ways of the new service before we can just go do it. This is a good way of living, because we do get restless with the same type of service or work after a while.

Ms. Alison:
Thank you, Harry. Next we have the topic of housing—who wants this one?

Rick:
I'll take it, Ms. Alison

Rick:
I have seen many pictures of the past eras that show various types of dwellings they had. Some were very beautiful and some were very poor. I have seen paper housing like the ones people lived in over in Asia and the really rundown buildings they called the slums like in New York City. However, today we cannot find any housing like that at all anywhere in the world. Everybody has a decent house to live in. People pick a house that fits the way they wish to live. I am glad we can provide the level of physical comfort today

so we do not see the homeless people that I have seen in pictures where they stood on the side of the street and asked for a handout of money so they could get some food to eat. I understand most of those people lived either out in the open or even in cardboard boxes at times. It appears that not very many people cared for the homeless and would look down upon them. That seems really heartless to me that so many people had to live that way--and the majority of the people that did not live that way did not care about those that were forced to live as homeless due to the lack of money.

Ms. Alison:
Thank you, Rick.

Ms. Alison:
Let's move on to science. Who wants to speak on this?

Ron:
I will, Ms. Alison

Ms. Alison:
I should have known you would volunteer, Ron. You are known as the computer geek of the school, aren't you? I am told that you will be one of our future scientists.

Ron:
Yes, Ms. Alison, I am studying to be a scientist, but I am not sure yet what area I will major in. As for this book, the section on science is fairly accurate in his interpretation of future developments. We do have a lot more advances that come out far more frequently than the era of money had. It is like he stated about the lack of restrictions when money was involved. We are not bound by the work it took back then to find and secure the money it would take to get a lab or new product started. One example of difference is back then the largest software maker was a company called Microsoft. They made most of the operating systems that computers ran on, but today a scientist made a completely new system while studying in school that has replaced that old system. This person could not have done that if he lived in the money era. He would not have been able to overtake such a large and well-funded monopolizing company because it would have taken a great deal of money that he did not have. I see he also understood about light technologies that would be developed in future times. Our communications units use light technology as a major part of their operation system. This along with the

biological storage cubes is what makes them so fast and able to store so much data.

Ms. Alison:
Thank you, Ron. Well, who will step up for this short section on people?

Kelly:
I will, Ms. Alison

Kelly:
From reading this paragraph I see that there was likely some concern about people dispersing into the world and not wanting to work. I guess that was because so many hated the jobs they felt they were tied to because they had to work to make money to live on. The part about them coming around to help is exactly what happened after some time passed and they did begin to see that it would require most or even all the people to pitch in and help turn that wheel of the physical world. It was not that long before they came around. Looking back on the massive amounts of people that worked in the jobs like the banks and government that no longer existed that made a large difference in the amount of people that were available to do the meaningful jobs that supported everything and everyone. Today we do not have any shortage of people to fill the roles of service for any of the required things we need. Our population is even bigger than it was back then, so we have to have more products to supply to our population. There are no big problems in our society for this area of life. I have tried to envision this time as if I were watching a movie where the movie goes back in time to show the audience what took place. Since I was not there it is a little hard to envision 100% accurately but the old movies and newsreels have helped me fill in the gaps.

Ms. Alison:
Thank you, Kelly. There is one more section to chapter three. Who will volunteer for the section on law?

Wayne:
I will. Ms. Alison. This is almost not worth mentioning because we do not have these kinds of dilemmas today. Law is a thing of the past and I am glad we have left it in the past. Since we have left all that behind, I think that section speaks for itself and we cannot compare that to today except to say we

no longer do anything even remotely like that to the people we all live with.

Ms. Alison:
I have to agree with you, Wayne. We need not spend much time going over this, except we do need to understand how it pertains to the area of control and deception they ravaged the people with. Please tell us what you remember of these two subjects, Wayne.

Wayne:
I guess the control part would be along the lines of them making these *laws* and then not teaching the masses about law so the ones that did know the laws would have an upper hand over the rest that did not understand the system of laws. This would put the masses into a position of lack because the system was so complicated to understand if one had no formal training. This would have created an intimidation factor in the masses. As for the ravaging part—they purposely would not teach the people about the laws, but I understand that they would say things like ignorance of the law is not an excuse for breaking a law. This was a deception. If the people were required to be knowledgeable about the laws then they should have been taught law in grade school and high school so there would be no ignorance of the law, as they demanded. This lack of teaching was apparently done on purpose so the system could easily take advantage of the people at will.

Ms. Alison:
That was good, Wayne. Now we will move onto chapter four. Allen, would you take the first section on this chapter?

Allen:
Yes, Ms. Alison.

Ms Alison:
Allen? Can you tell us what you recall from the future section?

Allen:
Yes. The first thing I see that is different is that they treated others at times in harsh ways by taking from them instead of assisting or helping others to learn and understand like we do today.

Ms. Alison:
Yes, Allen that is a good point. Go on.

Allen:
The next thing I noticed was that they had levels of acceptance between people over the amount of money each one had or could *earn*. Today, we honor all others as our equals. Ms. Alison, I have a question about this. Didn't this make people feel bad about themselves?

Ms. Alison:
Yes, Allen, some people even took their own lives and many times the life of another over the treatment from others and the torment they went through over money. Go on, Allen.

Allen:
Well, the next thing I see is that the author points to a far different situation when they get rid of money in that all things will become more of a winning situation for everybody. I think this is accurate for today's way of life. I also recall that they could only get things in life like a house or clothing that was in line with their ability to make money. I guess this was what drove some of them to the point of breaking; it seems that not all of them could have all the things we have today in our lives.

Ms. Alison:
Yes, Allen, some people were very limited in the quality of life they lived. Allen, please go on.

Allen:
I agree with the author's prediction about today where we just do our part in serving others and we can partake in all that is available as long as we do not over do it and take too much. My dad has an old car and a brand new car. Is that okay?

Ms. Alison:
Yes. The old car is probably quite old, isn't it?

Allen:
Yes, ma'am.

Ms. Alison:
Then it is probably a collector's car. There is nothing wrong in having

nostalgic property. Allen, may I ask how long did your dad keep the last car he had?

Allen:
We had that car for almost eight years. I guess that is not to far off from the author's suggestion on recycling cars. And, yes, we do take our old cars down to the auto replacement center and bring home a new one.

Ms. Alison:
What else do you recall?

Allen:
The last thing he writes of is the way we will run things in our generation. I agree with his evaluation of this. We do have a pretty good life now compared to what I have read about how they lived in the past and the harsh stresses they all endured. I guess that is all I remember.

Ms. Alison:
You did very well, Allen. However, there is one thing that I feel the author left out. He did not mention anything about mechanics of our day. We still have cars and they are mechanical as they have always been, granted they are better than the cars of the past, but never the less they are still mechanical and they do break down. Today we still have mechanics to repair them. After all, it would be foolish to recycle a new or even a fairly new car just because the guidance system or something broke down in it. Repairing it is far more economical and makes more sense than replacing the whole car over a minor problem even though we do not have to have money to replace a car.
The next section is transportation. Who wants to tackle this section?

Candy:
Ooo, I will, Ms. Alison.

Ms. Alison:
Thank you, Candy. Tell us what you learned from this in comparison to today.

Candy:
I wanted to answer this section because we went on a trip last year up into the mountains where there is no auto drive available because the roads were dirt. Ms. Alison, I promise this will tie in to the section. As I said my dad had to

actually drive the car himself on the dirt roads. I do not understand all that auto drive thingy stuff, but we were going down this hill on a very narrow part and the car started to go off the cliff. I think if the car didn't have that antigravity thingy we may have all been killed from the car going down the cliff. It was a long way down! I can tell you all that I do know that the antigravity feature is what helps make the car go and stop, but I don't understand it all that well. Dad said it did keep us from sliding down that cliff, though.

Ron:
Candy may I interject something about the antigravity thingy?
Candy:
Ok Ron

Ron:
That thingy you were describing is actually a propulsion unit that consists of magnetically charged molecules that actually push against gravity in much the same way two of the same magnet poles push away from each other in magnets. It works on a 15 to 48 degree angle effect to both lift and cause forward motion to whatever is attached to the unit. It also works in two directions on cars to move the car forward and backward. The greater the angle the quicker the car will move. This is created by a field of energy electrons passing through a transducer that converts and directs the moving particles to a very high-speed force of these electrons in the desired direction. The transducer converts this magnetic field in a sense into a gravity field of its own and that is then faced in a downward direction, which in turn acts to force the two fields of gravity like magnetics to push against each other. This process tends to moves a small amount of air in the same direction as the propulsion field to help with propulsion but this air movement only gives a minimal amount of help. It is like gravity against gravity but it starts with magnetics that are converted into a gravity field. I would also like to say that in the past like the time of the money era, scientists were just beginning to learn about the spinning molecules in a magnet. They understood little about how to harness them. Today we are able to control the raw power that was actually found in nature to be cruder than today's application of magnetics. To compare this from then to now would be like trying to burn crude oil in a motor that was designed to only ran on refined gasoline.

Ms. Alison:

Thank you for that description Ron. Candy. We are glad you were not injured in that potentially life-threatening experience, but is there anything else you can tell us about today in relation to the past?

Candy:
Oh, yes. The part where electricity was used in the past and today—we still have electricity for our lights, but I don't think it comes from a far off place. If I'm not mistaken, our electricity comes from that little box on the side of the house I think. Is that right?

Ms. Alison:
Yes, Candy, that is right. That box contains power cells that can last up to 150 years for the average house that is what provides our electricity. Your story tells it well enough pertaining to our technology today, but you have not compared it to the past. Can you elaborate on the differences a little?

Candy:
Yes, Ms. Alison. They did not have the antigravity and propulsion systems we have today that aid us in driving, so I guess their cars were not as safe as ours because if one of those old cars went off the cliff, it would have fallen and maybe killed those people. Hey, wait a minute, what about trains and planes?

Ms. Alison:
That's a good point, Candy. We have trains to move very large amounts of materials and products all over the country and we use planes to move products and people all over the world. They are also much safer and far more efficient in regards to energy consumption due to the developments we have made—some of which were predicted in this book. There are more advances in our society today, but they are not written of in this book, so I will not go into them. We just want to dwell on the past histories predictions. Thank you, Candy, for your story.

Ok let's move on to section three—communications. Ron, I want you to take this one since you are so fond of science and tinkering.

Ron:
Yes, Ms. Alison. The first thing I read about was the viruses. I have heard about them in science class. It seems that they were very common back when the Internet was created and for many years after that. They got them mostly in incoming emails. They would get an anonymous email that would carry an

infection virus with it. What I can tell you is that this must have stemmed from money.

As far as I can tell from this book and from my science class is that they sold their computer programs for money and many other people that were in that frame of mind copied and resold them or gave them to others for free. This infuriated the people that wrote the programs, which inspired them to write the viruses and try to spread them to the computers that had the copied free programs. This virus would then mess up the data and program files on those computers as an act of vengeance for having the program without buying it with money. Professor Ross says that the large virus elimination companies that made the virus removal programs which were used to repair the computers viruses found that it was very lucrative to also write viruses and distribute them as well because every time they did that, they would sell a lot of virus repair programs and make a lot of money. He said they did this in secret by hiring people from another part of the world to write and send out the viruses for them.

Ms. Alison:
Ron, there was another reason people wrote viruses--that was because they were wronged by an employer or they were angry about the computer business or they just didn't like themselves or others very well. So they would try to mess up other people's computers by sending out these viruses. This is all intriguing, but we do not have any such monsters today. Why would anyone want to? There is nothing in it for them to do this and they would be tracked and caught instantly anyway if someone did do this today. Ron, please continue.

Ron:
As for the government, we all know that ours is much smaller today and there is no need to spy on anyone because there is no money or greed that anyone can gain from. Everything today is free, so communications or traveling anywhere in the world is not an issue anymore. We have downsized so much of our government that there is virtually no power left in it for anyone to control others with. We also monitor the government to make sure it cannot create anything we have not all agreed to in society. We have learned from our past not to let anything like that get out of hand and take control of people again.

Ms. Alison:

Ron, tell us about your watch and communications toys.

Ron:
Oh yeah. With the chip that is in my grandpa's old Rolex watch I can load and watch a holographic movie on my wrist anywhere I am at any time. I can also project it on a wall. I can make calls and watch the movie at the same time as well as share it with the person I am calling. I can store our entire five years of class papers, schedules meetings and a lot more in our communication chips. I can talk to the chip and it will answer my questions based on what is stored in it, like what class I have next week at 3 p.m. I can have it access the world net for information not stored in the chip and it will extrapolate and answer my questions and also store the new info for a later time if needed.

The chip is an intelligent chip that will find exactly what I want without me looking through dozens of pages of text, like that old antique computer in my technology class does. I guess it is from the era of money where all it could do was search for a word or phrase on a page and then bring back all the pages it found with that word. The user would still have to read through many pages of text to find if there was anything there he was looking for. That must have been time consuming and somewhat frustrating.

This chip in my communicator is something they did not have in what they called the public sector when this book was written. They did have organic storage devices in the military but they were not as good as what we have now. Today it will read all that it finds and then bring exactly what I was looking for instantly; I do not have to read all that stuff that they used to have to do. Oh, yeah, that old computer has several big bulky parts to it: it has a viewing screen, a keyboard, a mouse and a big box for the processor chip and then it all has to be connected together with cables and connected to electricity from an outside source in order for it to work.

The next part of this section talks about burdening all the people for the costs of the limited Internet communications they had back then. We are not burdened because everything is at no cost except our service and labor to help the whole of humanity. This greed they talk about sounds like a form of competition, but it seems they had no rules to play that game, so there were many losers and only a few winners.
Wow! Just thinking of how this must have been makes me a little dizzy.

Ms. Alison:

Very perceptive of you, Ron. That is exactly correct on the winners and losers comment you just made.

Ron:
Ms. Alison, I can see where the government would want to monitor all the people in this era–because they were afraid of being attacked from someone that wanted to destroy them as well as other innocent people. It seems that the government was more afraid than most people were; I guess that must have been because they provoked the attacks in the first place.

Ms. Alison:
That was very good, Ron. I am glad you paid attention to that section. The day is running short, so let's move on to the next section for today. Do I have a volunteer for the security section?

Rick:
Yes, Ms. Alison. I will take this section.

Ms. Alison:
Ok, Rick.

Rick:
I agree with Ron about the last section on security. They must have had to watch their computers very closely. It seems that they developed this global communications tool, and then many people wanted to use it to conspire to do harm to others somehow. What I see is that they must have sent messages back and forth over this Internet where they would plan acts of destruction. Am I right, Ms. Alison?

Ms. Alison:
Yes, that is part of it. They would also share things in secret through codes. You could find information on how to make bombs and weapons on the Internet easily at first. This is part of the reason monitoring and security was developed.

Rick:
Why would the governments create these attacks upon themselves?

Ms. Alison:

Because they just did not know they were doing this at all--they thought in their time that they were doing some good by policing everything to the extent they did, rather than find the root of the problem and get rid of it. Rick, we've covered much of this already so let's move on to the other parts of this section.

Rick:
I remember the rebelliousness part that was created by the use of money. I do not remember having to rebel for anything other than when my mom said I could not have three cheeseburgers for lunch last month. I guess that wasn't really a rebellion. I guess what I am trying to say is that I do not understand what a rebellion really is. I think it is when a person wants to harm another because someone made a limitation or forced something on them first or something.

Ms. Alison:
Yes, Rick, that is pretty good, but let me say that it went much deeper than that. The rebellious nature came from many years of oppressive treatment by those that the people looked up to for security, protection, and a good lifestyle. Both the people and the government they created did not understand the root of what was creating the massive amounts of rebellion. Ok you may continue, Rick.

Rick:
I do understand that we all live on this planet together, and as a whole planet of people we need to work together to make it all go around smoothly or we could wind up going back into the chaos of the past.

Ms. Alison:
Do you realize, Rick, that they thought they had peace back then? They called it lack of war. Can you imagine that? If there were no wars in the world they thought they were at peace. All they really had was a lack of war for a short time until the next one would break out. They did not understand that peace was the understanding that came from within each person on how to honor each other and play well together. They also thought that other cultures were so different than them that it must not be a good thing to have that culture on the earth, so they would try to wipe them out. And, of course, there were greedy motivations as they took their land while attempting to wipe them out.

Rick:

Ms. Alison?

Ms. Alison:
Yes, Rick.

Rick:
About laws~I have seen pictures of the buildings they used to have to keep all the laws in with all those books. How could they have made so many laws?

Ms. Alison:
I think we have already covered the how part, but what is most important is we do not have these law books anymore except a few in museums. The rest were recycled for new paper. What else do you remember from this section, Rick?

Rick:
I remember the part about free will. I totally agree with the author's interpretation of this topic. In fact, that is what our society holds in high esteem today. The next part is where the system of that era did not care for its people, only what it could take from them. That must have been barbaric for the people of that time. We have no such thing today that I can recall. Ms. Alison, they used to put people in jails in huge quantities, didn't they?

Ms. Alison:
Yes, they did. Thank God we don't still do this to our people today. We still have detention facilities, but they are not used to the extent that they were back then. Today we only hold a person if they are having trouble in some way that may be a danger to the others. We then evaluate their psychological issues and help them learn why they have these issues and help them to heal. They are then free to go home. It all takes a few weeks under our understanding of the psyche. Our people are not held in a cell and treated with such anger and disrespect like back then. It is more like a nice hotel; all the people that service there are well educated in psychology. Rick, you are down almost to the end of this section. Please go on.

Rick:
I went to the archives last night and found one of the old Star Trek movies. We all watched it last night. My dad said he used to get these from the

archives and watch them sometimes when he was little. I stumbled on one show where the ship went back in time to an earlier time and the captain said to one of the people from the past that they no longer used money in the 24th century and that they worked to better themselves rather than try to get ahead of others or something like that. That old movie was a bit hokey, but I thought it was still interesting for something made so long ago. I think we have something similar to their Prime Directive, but a bit different. They never said what the Prime Directive was, but I think it must have been not to interfere in other cultures; this non-interference is what we do today. In that sense the book is fairly accurate for the way we live today.

Ms. Alison:
I think you are right, Rick, on that part. There is one more thing I wish to add in regard to the soul. We all know that the soul is highly regarded and our purpose on earth is to evolve and better ourselves in the ways we can through our life's path. For the era of this book, that was so very restricted to such a degree that this almost did not happen for many people at all. Down through history man has searched for the "*seat of the soul*" as it was often called. Man did not know where this was or even if it was in the human body. Today we know that the portion of the soul that resides in the human form is located in a small pocket just behind the heart. It cannot be seen, as the soul is still invisible to the human eye.
Well, class, I see our time is almost up for today. We will resume this tomorrow.

[The next day.]
Ms. Alison:
Good morning again, class. Are we all ready for the day? Adel, would you like to start off the day with this next section about freedom?

Adel:
Yes, Ms. Alison. This section deals with freedom of speech. I noticed that some words were said to be bad to use or maybe they were banned from use though they were a part of the culture or language and were still written in the dictionaries of the time. The one word the author used, as an example was *fuck*. He also said the use of these words caused the rebellious nature of the people to use these words more frequently than they would have if they were not restricted from use. I think that if we were told when we were little not to say certain things, we too may want to use them in spite, as they seem to have done according to the description of this section, especially if the one that

told me not to use it was using it. This word he used just means to me the same as sex, intercourse, reproduction, etc. I don't see anything wrong with this word. I guess it's because we were not told that some words were not good to use while we're growing up. I understand the author's point here. He is trying to say if you have it as part of your language, you should accept it because it is a part of the society, which means it is a part of you and the culture, besides this word in particular is a partial description of how procreation of the species happens.. So I don't see why they would think it was bad. Most likely it had to do with religious teachings.

I have already addressed the Lord's name in vain part in what I just said. I think that is the same thing as with the other words. I like the way the author thinks. I also think it has something to do with the way we are today. If people had started to think in less restrictive terms as we have over time, dropping the old ways of thinking, then our current evolution would be even further along than it is now.

Ms. Alison:
Thank you, Adel. This section was shorter than some of the others. However, I think you are exactly right the people did change their way of thinking and acting over time, otherwise we would not be who we are today. Evolution is a slow process in terms of earth time, but to the cosmos and the age of the universe it is a wink of an eye.

This next section on medical issues is about the same length. Serina, we haven't heard from you yet.

Serina:
Yes, Ms. Alison. From reading this part I see that they cut parts of the body out or off or something that seems a little strange to us today, since we mostly heal by use of vibrational and light technologies that repair the bad cells from within the body and even within the diseased cell itself. I do understand that they did not understand the body very well. If we think back to the earliest days, the caveman knew nothing at all compared to what the era of money people knew. I see the slow progression of technological advancements. I think the future people will think we are stupid for the way we do things because they will have gone way beyond our technologies. He did hint at the healing tools that our doctors use today in the area of light and sound vibration, so he was close in that regard in predicting a little bit of our way of

life today. I have not studied biology, so I don't know anything about the medical tools of today.

Ms. Alison:
Yes, Serina, he did talk some about the tools, but did you notice he wasn't very specific in his descriptions of our technologies?

Serina:
No, Ms. Alison. I didn't notice that.

Ms. Alison:
It appears to me from reading the rest of this book that he intended his explanations this way on purpose. He was leaving the advancement of technologies open to possibility. In other words, he did not specify any limitation so that no one who might have read this book would limit his or her advancements and ideas. He hinted at a direction and then left it open to the imaginations of the developers of the new tools. Or he just really did not know what he was talking about. What do you think, Serina?

Serina:
I think from what I have read of this book, maybe the first part you said about his intentions would be more accurate. I also think he may not have been that scientific and maybe not able to interpret the information he was drawing on to put it into words.

Ms. Alison:
Yes Serina that may be as well, what about the next part, Serina?

Serina:
Oh, you mean balance of the body. Well I can stand on one toe, is that good enough?

Class chuckles:

Ms. Alison:
No.

Serina:
Okay. I am sorry, Ms. Alison. He was referring to the way the body operates as a whole and complete unit. Last year we learned about the balance of the

body's system as a whole in health class to prevent getting ill and to ward off old age for a long time. From this section it seems that the radiation they used to heal was throwing bodies way out of balance because it killed the diseased cells as well as the healthy ones, so it must have really been a bad thing to do to the body. Since I don't know what that must have been like, I don't think I can make a fair comparison of today and then.

I do understand the thought processes that can make a person feel bad. Over time if we were to stay that way, we would get sicker and sicker because the patterns of the mind would spiral down and then the body would follow the mind's lead and deteriorate, and become ill. We understand that is how aging works, first the mind believes the body must grow old then the body follows the beliefs of the mind and starts to deteriorate until it dies.

Ms. Alison:
Serina, that was quite good, thank you. Let's see whom have I not called? William, it seems to be your turn now.

William lets here what you know about recycling:
Okay, Ms. Alison. I don't know about the past so much, but I do know we do have many recycled products–even some wood is recycled today. The walls and floor of our gym are made from recycled woods. From what I understand, it is like melting paper back down into a liquid and adding some new compounds to make the old wood very durable and resilient to weather and even somewhat flexible compared to tree wood. Professor Ross said in science class that some old tire rubber is even added like in the gym floor to cushion and allow for a good bounce for jumping during basketball. Last summer I was going to help at the car plant. I was even looking forward to it because I wanted to tear apart some cars, but my dad asked me to help my aunt in her bookstore so I went their instead. But I plan to do the car thing next summer.

Ms. Alison:
Thank you, William. We can all see the advantages of caring for our planet, can't we? Recycling has come a long way from the money era. We would not have the level of recycling we do if we were still in the money era.

Enough said on this subject. It's time to go to the next topic. However, we are going to skip the next two since I think everybody has a good understanding. And we have mostly covered them earlier anyway. So let's move on to critics.

I am going to ask for a volunteer on this one.

Amy:
May I, Ms. Alison?

Ms. Alison:
Yes, Amy, you may.

Amy:
I have read this section and I find that the explanation of how greed started and grew seems to be interesting. Further, I agree that this must have been ingrained deeply because from the caveman era to the king era, sometime before the industrial revolution period, there was still a fighting type of survival in many ways, as I understand history. I also believe that we have lived past lives in these eras ourselves and we are our own ancestors. Today we feel deep down inside that, that way of existence is and was a stepping-stone to the future and our current understandings that we need to live with each other instead of trying to crush one another over anything. We have evolved to this level at great cost to our mental and emotional past ancestral sufferings.

As for the critics saying this cannot work, I disagree as we are living proof that it does work. After the education and adjusting we read about and what stories we are told by our grand parents, we can see it works. I like the part where the author was told to come up with a better way and then many years later he did and wrote this book because of it. It appears that we too are critics of this book because we are using and picking it apart in this class. Ms. Alison, was the marshal law put into action as he writes here?

Ms. Alison:
I cannot answer that because I have never found any information to that effect that would pertain to this timeframe in history. If it did happen it was kept very low key and not disclosed to the public like they did after a court case where the defendant won the case but the courts did not want the win to be public knowledge, so they sealed the cases. However, I can tell you that the critics and the government did make their protests and attempts to change the way the people were beginning to think and act as time went on. There is evidence that some resistance was raised from the system for a time before it all fell apart.
Amy, what else did you get from this in relation to today?

Amy:
I think that things did go somewhat as predicted in this book. It had to change because the people were changing, which is evident in the fact that this book got written during the time period that it was written about. I also think the book was overdue because of all the control and how people hated the way they lived for so long but most didn't really realize it.

Ms. Alison:
Well, class, that wraps up this section. I want to read to you this next part that deals with a combination of the *Critics* section and the next chapter on evolution. Then we will go onto chapter six evolution of the soul.

[Ms. Alison reads from the book.]

As with any new idea, there are always negative critics. It is expected that some will say this is an idealistic approach to an age-old problem. I say if you study the effects of this approach, you may begin to realize the problems of money, and the way life would be without money.

Here is a real life example taken from my own past. Two very different types of parents raised me. My mother was the hard-handed type if you crossed her in any way. She would either give a swift smack across the face or a stick across the ass. On the other hand, my father was the gentle type with light instruction who then let you learn from your mistakes, as he put it. He felt you would learn better that way and subsequently you would become far less rebellious and more respectful. He thought this approach would also make one more susceptible to listening to their elders after a few mistakes of their own.

I do not do the *mother* thing and I do not do the *father* thing. Instead I have taken from both, but I do lean more toward the *father* side of things. I do have a little of the frustration of the mother side, but without the physical contact she liked so much. This example shows evolution in how I changed and learned from both sides and then chose the gentler of the two. I still get my buttons pushed as most of us do in this era (and sometimes quite easily). The button pushing is usually in connection with money. I have moved away from the old and embraced the new ways that I see for our future. Look at yourself-what is in your heart? If you are past the heavy macho years, do you really have any malice inside you toward others that would cause you to intentionally do harm to others? Or do you not sometimes just react to stimulus with anger when you were done an injustice or have been treated with anger from another?

My little story above did not deal directly with the use of money, but I think you get the idea of evolution and moving from the harsh (money era) to the gentler (no money era) way of dealing with the past limitations, greed, control and restrictions that (with our permission) money can place in one's society. I hope by now you can better understand the restrictions, control, and limitations of using money.

If you agree with this statement, then you can begin to see the point of this book and the way it is going to be sometime in the future. You can begin to measure the evolution of your own heart and mind within your own life. Each generation takes this a little or a lot further. This takes me to the next topic of evolution.

[Ms. Alison addresses the class.]

Ms. Alison:
Class, as you can see, the author is trying to convey a message about the deeper understanding of all people regarding an inner sense of understanding and evolution of the mind and soul in an expanded future understanding of other generations. Class, your reading assignment for tonight is to read chapters six and seven.

Chapter Six

Evolution of the human and the soul

For the purpose of this book, the evolution of the soul is between the person and the *all that is* or God. This brings a law to mind (that pertains to the way law was meant to be in the beginning days of the USA) that was written for what is called a *sovereign* before the fraud of the early mid-nineteenth century took place. At that time all people were sovereigns. A sovereign only lasted in this country from the beginning up until 1933, at which time Citizens were reverted back to the slavery of the English parliament, the government, and, mostly, the banks. Of course, this was done in secrecy and by design to re-enslave the population. This law states non-interference from the government on its people by any state or nobility. Below is the latest version of this law. Under today's laws no persons are considered a sovereign by the government. As you may notice in this law, a sovereign is a foreigner to the current incarnation of the united States of America. (And, by the way, the capitalization for the USA is correct as it pertains to this law.) That is because the Sovereign is not a corporation as most other people are. This corporation status occurred after the birth certificate was mandated. In light of this act of fraud upon the people of this country, non-Sovereigns cannot use the following law and the state and federal governments have control of the people as if they were a corporation like any other business. The federal government, according to the Constitution of the united States, was never to have control of the people directly. The people were protected by the states from the feds, but that all changed in 1933. However, many people of this latter part of the money era are using a redemption process to take their Sovereignty back from the government. This is/was yet another step in our evolution toward a non-money society.

RESPONSIBILITY DISCLAIMER UNDER U.C.C. 3-501. UNDER TITLE 42 U.S.C. 1986 FOR KNOWLEDGE OF THE LAW, VENUE AND JURISDICTION OF ALL ACTIONS/CASES RELATING TO THIS CONTRACT ARE UNDER COMMON LAW JURISDICTION OF THE TITLE 4 U.S.C.: 1 AMERICAN FLAG OF PEACE OF THE united STATES OF AMERICA, REFERENCED UNDER PRESIDENTIAL EXECUTIVE ORDER 10834, AND UNDER ARTICLE (6) SECTION (3), OATH OF FIDUCIARY OFFICERS OF THE COURT, AND UNDER ARTICLE (IV) (4) SECTION (3), NO "state" (JUDGE) SHALL CREATE A STATE (AREA OF THE BAR), AND united STATES CODE ANNOTATED 11: NO "FOREIGN STATE" (LAW OF THE FLAG) SHALL HAVE JURISDICTION OVER A SOVEREIGN CITIZEN IN PARTY, AND ARTICLE (1) SECTION (9),AMENDMENT 13: NO TITLES OF NOBILITY (ESQUIRES) UNDER ANY FOREIGN FLAG JURISDICTION AND IN BREACH OF THE TREATY OF TITLE 28 U.S.C. 1605 "FOREIGN SOVEREIGN IMMUNITY ACT OF October 21, 1976 AND IN BREACH OF THE CONSTITUTION OF THE united STATES OF AMERICA, WILL BE ALLOWED IN THE JURISDICTION OF THE CASE. BREACH OF CONTRACT BY ANY PARTY WILL CAUSE SANCTIONS UNDER FEDERAL RULES OF CIVIL PROCEDURE RULE 16(t), WHEN THE CONSTITUTION OF THE united STATES OF AMERICA IS SURRENDERED FOR A FOREIGN STATE/POWER, AND BREACH OF CONTRACT OF OATH OR AFFIRMATION FOR THE united STATES OF AMERICA, THEN CHARGES FOR PERJURY OF OATH (TITLE 18 U.S.C. 1621), CONSTRUCTIVE TREASON, AND FALSE SWEARING WILL BE BROUGHT AGAINST THE OFFICERS OF THE COURT. THE CONSTITUTION OF THE united STATES OF AMERICA IS MADE A PART OF THIS CONTRACT BY REFERENCE AND IN A "REAL TIME" "PRESENT

TENSE" STATE OF BEING.

What these above collection of laws mean is that the government secretly and without your permission created a fictitious person using your given name from the birth certificate that was suddenly required at all hospitals in 1933. The system always gives as a remedy to any new law(s) before the new encroaching laws are put on the books. They do this to save face at a later time in case they get caught with their pants down. If you look at it from a certain perspective this avenue of remedy is a good thing for the Citizens. When they stop doing this it will be a matter of dire consequences for the population. This law have since been requiring you; the living man or woman, to pay for all that is charged and taxed to that fiction. You as the living breathing man or woman are not that corporate fictional person. You do not owe anything they say you owe. The banks perpetrate the biggest of all cons going on in the money era. Why do they wish to control? It is unknown for sure, but I am certain it's been going on for so long now that even the original instigators heirs do not know why this is or was ever set into motion against the people of this planet.

Enough of the legal mumbo jumbo--all that confusing junk is old energy for an old era of time anyway that will be no more in the new era. To change all that highly confusing stuff is to just turn away and live as we were meant to live and evolve.

Evolution is a constant in this universe. All things move forward to somewhere in time while existing only in the now moment. Nothing exists in any time frame other than now, in this moment. They never go backwards, even though I know some people that seem to think in backwards terms. Our evolution is the progression of our learning over many, many lifetimes. Some do not think that there is a reincarnation, but I ask those of you who think this way to do a past life regression and see how much you can remember of living in poor conditions or in a castle or living off the land with animal skins as clothing, etc. You can go back and do this for many hundreds of lifetimes. This will prove your remembrance of your reincarnation many times over and over.. You are your own ancestors. You lived many times and brought forward the encoded memories of the past experiences with you from life to life. You just cannot remember them in your conscious mind because you are not meant to. This way, you will go through life each time not knowing of past lives and thus living a whole new set of experiences to take with you as stored memories to the next life and so on. These experiences are stored on a soul level and always carried with you. Your subconscious mind accesses these memories and helps direct one to move in the current life acquiring experiences the soul deems necessary for your personal evolution. If you knew what you did in one or more of your past lives, you would automatically tend to live that again and again each new lifetime. That would limit one's evolution from what it was meant to be by the *all that is*.

Here is a little test for you, the reader. Think about a situation in your life that you did not want to happen and even tried to change, but you just for some reason could not make a difference. No matter what you did, that situation just would not change. Here is the validation answer: it was directed by your subconscious mind to be necessary for you to go through that experience because it is or was a crucial part of your current life this time around. It is a necessity for your evolution at this time. This also holds true for something you wanted but just could not achieve, no matter what you tried.

Think about this for a moment: knowing how people are, even today in our so-called advanced state of living, we see people that tend to get stuck in a rut very easily. Just think what we would be like if we could remember all the past lives we have had, the ways we lived then would be carried over and the rut would be deep and we would only be about half the distance or less than we are now in our evolution. Just how far along the path of evolution do you think we would be today if we remembered our past lives? Did you also know you are drinking the same water the dinosaurs drank?

The level of accomplishment one could achieve as they were controlled by the use of money was greatly limited. Some did make their way to the top of the money ladder, as it was called. But those people usually did so by stepping on and using the efforts of others for personal gain, taking without a conscience from many other people to get up that ladder. This kind of treatment toward other people limits the evolution process of the one doing the ladder stepping because it is at the expense of others. The future is not going to be like this; instead it will provide a way of living equally with respect and honor for all other people. Without money to take from one another, there will not be the level of taking from others as there is now. There will still be desire for a level of comfort in living, but all things will be free. There will be no need to control others anymore. If a worldly comfort is not available the people will get together and build that comfort for themselves and others.

If one honors another person even in the money era, one is not likely to harm the person they honor. When we move into this system of honor, we will no longer war, hate, argue, fight, degrade, oppress, subdue, limit, control or hurt others for any reason. They in turn will do the same for and to all others. This illustrates a more authentic meaning of the word *peace*, but it is still not the full explanation of peace. Peace is not the absence of war as is portrayed today in the money era. True peace goes far beyond the absence of war. It exists on an inner level of harmony within each person. It is the true knowing of oneself first, and then when you fully know yourself you will automatically know others. There is much I can say about this experience of peace, but that will be held for another section of this book (or even another book all together).

The standards of living in the *now future*, as it would be well known by the students in this future class and the whole of society, are such that everything is perceived far differently than in the past. The new era lives in harmony within the self and sees others as equals and they all carry a respect for one another deep within their minds, hearts, and souls, knowing who they truly are inside. That knowing gives them the understanding of who everyone and everything else is simultaneously.

Back in the money era people did not know who they were as beings of a higher order that were on earth to evolve in a physical sense—the *grand plan* as it has been called. This has changed greatly in recent times because, like a falling object, it will gain momentum until it reaches maximum velocity, which comes in a very short time. You could say that time has sped up lately. So, we could be at that maximum velocity or are about to reach it soon. Our evolution from the money era is reaching this velocity faster than ever, so much so that future generations will evolve even faster than now.

I have stated what things may be like in the future of our existence, but that is still only a probability. It may go another way all together or it may go exactly as I've written here. We do not know for sure. I do know if it stays the same, as it is now, we will self-destruct in a relatively short matter of time. And I say this with only a little time in mind, possibly two to four generations, maybe less before this destruction. The higher probability is to move out of this old energy era of money and move upward in understanding. There may be some upheavals along the path to the new era, which will be necessary for us to get

from the old to the new way.
There will be a quantum leap on September 18th 2007. After 2007 the dynamics will change considerably. Instead of energetic forces opposing each other to create vibration and therefore reality, it will be that neutral energy is activated and expands/contracts all at the same time. That will create the new reality.
It is difficult to say how fast this will happen after this date. But it will bring amazing changes in technologies and medicines, and the healing arts. People will have access to whole new types of capabilities in the work they do with others, especially in homeopathic healing. Then later we will see major improvements in the technology of the mainstream medical fields. There will be no noticeable differences from the day before to the day after this takes place but the energies will shift greatly. This shift will enable many changes down the road of humanity.

The new earth

The new earth is a formation of gasses that is now visible in the distance of space that scientist are beginning to see with the Hubble telescope. It is a non-solid mass of a very different energy than most solid planets. The characteristics of this planet are very different from the physical planet of earth. This planet does not have many souls inhabiting it yet but the number is growing. As more humans become enlightened they become eligible to move to this new earth when they leave the 3 dimensional Earth.

This planet will not have the things we have on the 3rd dimension like police, wars, crime, cars, laws, houses, or even a physical body. The beings of that planet exist as a conscious intelligent energy only. They will have the ability to create anything they wish instantly by thinking it and it will be so. Example if one or more beings decide to play the role of a human they can just think it and they will be in physical human form again, creating what would appear to be a physical reality to play in. They will be able to play the roles just like humans do on the 3-D earth like go to a movie, have sex, eat a great meal etc. when they are done with the role playing they can drop the physical form just as easily as they created it. This is done by these being just for the fun and experience of having it again, but on a temporary basis only.

What this planet does have is a lighter mass of creation that looks like a gaseous formation to the human eye, but to the energy beings it will look similar to the earth of the 3-D. it will have a minimal gravity and the sun light will be somewhat different than that of the old earth.

Beliefs, a point of view

We create our world from what we believe on a deeper subconscious level, but not as we think and not so much from our conscious levels. Our beliefs about God are a basis we use to form our beliefs.

We use the stars to formulate beliefs too, but we must remember when we are taking the beliefs of the astrologer who believes something different than the astrologer down the street or around the world. This is a poor place to put our trust.

Travel

As humans we travel all the time both in our waking state and especially in our sleep states. We travel all over the universe and beyond on a daily basis. We do this on many different levels (dimensions). On the physical level we are highly restricted in movement and are placed under all kinds of requirements with paying money and filing paper of permissions like passports with various agencies to prove who you are and where you are going, to or from. The requirements placed upon us is burdensome, we have to tell them why, where, when, how long, and declare items we are carrying with us. This is always placed upon others by another living being(s) that are also living beings in the physical the same as us. Why do men try so hard to restrict other so much? There is no good and valid reason for this. All humans are of the same source of God energy, so how is it we place so much restriction upon each other? Do we have a right to do this against another's free will?

One valid cause for this is due to the fact we do not see each other as we truly are, we do not see that the same energy in others is the same within each of us. That same energy is the source of the *all that is* and is identical in each of us no matter who or what you are.

Spiritual groups Are they really all that spiritual

As a member of several spiritual groups over the course of my life I have found that most of the individuals that belong to these groups are really not all that spiritual when it gets right down to the day to day grind of the human condition. Life is grueling for many on the earth plain due to the developments of the 3rd dimensional reality over time dealing with balancing personal growth, jobs, family, necessities of taking care of the physical form with clothing, food and shelter. Then there is a great deal more heaviness dealing with greed of wealth and power over another to obtain that wealth. Couple all this with relationships and the breaking of them on an emotional level that can drive the mind in sane at times. All of this takes its toll on the good nature of the soul and mind in ways that create an inner hostility toward other well-meaning souls. It is funny to witness the hostility of someone that usually exudes a very spiritual nature most of the time. We all have anger buttons that can still be pushed from time to time. When those spiritual people get angry they can seem quite hostile in there words and actions toward other souls on the same path. This seems to be an out of character way for a light worker to behave but it happens all the time and is just as ugly as other people fighting that are not of like minds.

The facts behind all this are very numerous and not worth going into because that would only lead this book down another road that this author cares not to journey. The truth of this book is to point to the fact that we are like we are because we have gotten off coarse a long time ago in our evolution. We have fallen deeper into the illusion of the third dimension than we should have and now we are lost so deep that we think the third dimension is very real, so real that we think this is all there is to life. Or should I say existence. We exist on many levels and dimensions simultaneously but we no longer know it because of the depths we have sunk into the third dimensional reality. Again we create that reality by the beliefs we carry in our minds.

Disconnect

In order to move up in spiritual awareness one must disconnect the self from the mass-consciousness of the third dimensional thinking and allow the self to rise into the vibration of the new energy. This must be a conscious intent or command of the mind and all the different levels of the self. There are many levels of beliefs that we must release in order to move away from the old energies and upward into the new energy of existence of the new world. In this one must also block the effects and constant bombardment from the world at large from thwarting ones own efforts. Fear is an underlying conditional form of resistance that is programmed into the belief system of everyone so a separate intent must also be given to eliminate the lever of fear that exists at an even deeper level than the issues themselves. As the self and mind bring the issues to light, they will be released. One way to accomplish this could be to use visualization techniques along with a command or intent towards oneself to gather all levels of the mind, higher consciousness, super consciousness, spirit and all the angelic helpers that surround oneself to work together for the purpose of revealing and releasing the issues of beliefs and blockages of old energy thinking. After or during the command/intent process, an example of a visualization may be something like seeing yourself as a form in any shape you wish with layers of paint that are cracked and pealing, then see a force coming up under the form and breaking all the paint chips away from the form, blowing them out into space. Then see the chips being transformed into white light by a blast from a point in space hitting the chips directly and exploding them.

Then as needed see a second layer doing the same thing for as many levels as needed and as often as needed to go deeper into the many levels of self until the process brings the required realizations of enlightenment to move away from the mass-consciousness and into the new levels of the new energy. This process will enlighten and bring one out of the old outmoded ways and into the new understanding of the evolving new earth. This process will do many other things as long as the individual is of a spiritually conscious awareness and continues to maintain an upward development into the new energies. Among them are the ability to transmute illness and disease from the body, it will allow one to walk in and out of the physical body at will, one will never die and the individual will also be able to transform molecular energy from one form to another like turning rocks into gold.

The journey to enlightenment could easily be seen as a treasure hunt. The one on the journey could view themselves as a treasure hunters. The treasure is the discovery of the divine self or the allowing of the decent of the divine self into the physical being while still in the physical body. This is the goal and teachings of spirit today. We will do far greater things than Christ did in the time he walked the earth. It is best to be with others of like mind during this process. Joining a spiritual group that is on a path of ascension will accomplish this.

Your story
We all have deep rooted programming and concerns that seem to be our safety net. We feel that we cannot let go of this because we might fall apart if we did. As a spiritual man, woman or child we must let these programming issues go in order to evolve up the scale of evolution. Why hold onto our old

stories? We believe so much that this story is what and who we are that we go into fear at the mere thought of letting go of our identity. This seems like an outrage to just let go, maybe we will cease to be, or we would explode or maybe we would become a wondering idiot.

The truth is that we are so used to these stories over so many lifetimes that it has become all we know, even though we do evolve. The past life stories are genetically carried over from one life to the next by our soul memories and stored in our DNA. These memories are usually not conscious to us in the life we currently live in but do sometimes surface in our dreams where we may dream of being killed by a guillotine or drowning or being a king etc. the ones that do surface from time to time are usually of a dramatic or intense traumatic nature. Those past lives do affect us on an unconscious level and tend to direct out lives for a resolution of old past issues. The way it comes about in the current life is that we are directed on a higher level to enter into certain situations in life where we re-live an issue in order to release and settle the past unresolved feelings that were not released in the prior lives. This is also known as karma. An example of this may be in direct relation to the one you may be married to, or it may be a short relationship that came and went quickly but was either really good or really bad for you. This could have been however brief a necessary experience for you to resolve and release a small issue from something you and the other person may have had in common in a past life. This can come in many forms like the work you do in this life may be related to past issues or where you live now and/or where you were born in the world.

The evolution rate however has been very slow up until now taking millions of years to make even the smallest differences. What we are being asked is to let go of all the old lifetimes of ourselves and return back to the underlying true selves of when we first came through the great void as pure energy, but still remain in human form at this time. Our true selves are still and always with us buried under all those stories. It is our foundation, the story is just an overlay that has been there so long and grown so large that we cannot see the foundation from our current perspective. Releasing the stories will bring forth a new and wondrous angelic being of great magnitude and brilliance. Now wouldn't this be far greater than the drudgery of the story you currently exist in. Evolution will come forth but at a different pace for each soul. Some will take the new tracks on upward and some will take the old slower tracks. You must decide which set of tracks you want to ride on. There is going to be a split in consciousness in the year 2007 and the tracks will be parted at that time. The old will continue as they have been for all these eons and the new will be the teachers of the old that are starting to wake up in the coming years. This is why we will remain in human form after the split and shedding of the old stories. Our jobs will be that of spirit's job now and then the spiritual teachers we have will be our students in the physical world.

Feeling

Have you ever wondered why no matter how much you think about something or wish for that something or pray or maybe beg for it that it seems to never manifest for you. Well so have I and the answer that finally dawned on me is that I was doing it all wrong. For many decades, I tried thinking about what I wanted in many different ways only to find they never happened. The problem was that I was doing just that "thinking" instead of "FEELING" as it turns out the only way to get something to happen that you may want is to feel it within yourself and then it will happen. You must know it first within the feeling center in order to make it so.

To explain how I came to this understanding has to do with my studies of the spiritual understandings and a situation that has occurred many times in my life but only from time to time. What would occur at these times was something I thought was coming from my mind as a knowing feeling that always seemed to happen, usually right away. However the reality of this was that, that knowing was not from my mind but instead it was from my feeling center that I found in the heart center, which is physically located in the chest area of the body. Now this feeling center is directly linked to the mind so it appears to be coming from the mind. The mind is the analytical portion of the consciousness and immediately interprets what it feels that the feeling center has put forth. This chatter tells you that something good or bad is about to happen, but only after the feeling center puts forth its feelings and or findings of a potential situation that is pending.

Fear is a feeling that we all get, and most of us can relate to that as not coming from the mind. This originates and is felt in the stomach area for the most part. You know that sinking feeling well by this time in your life. It does not come from the mind at all. As all of this is saying we cannot think our way to make something, we want to happen at will we can only feel our way to make something happen.

Because we have been so programmed to think in our heads, we are virtually shut off from our feelings center and the ability to just know the answers to our needs and desires at will. The next question is how do we feel at will on a chosen subject to make positive change for ourselves.

The answer to this question can be found in the heart center by feeling what is in that center without thinking. Take your thoughts about what you want and transfer it to your heart center and let it run with it for a few days and a new feeling will come back about the issue or desire. If you are unable to do the transfer then make a command of the mind. Say to yourself I command myself, my higher self, my conscious mind, my subconscious mind, my super-conscious mind and my guides/angels to release the issues or blocks that I am holding that are keeping me from this ??/whatever it is, desire or experience you wish to now feel or create. Making this command in this way can bring in help from other higher sources that will bring about the realization and a releasing of the blocks that keep you from being able to feel in the heart center.

When you can feel at will you can make great changes in your life and surroundings. You can transform life into a better experience for yourself. Bad things will drop away automatically when you feel a better situation for yourself. People, jobs locations that are holding you back or causing you stress and dissatisfaction will leave your life making it better for <u>you</u> all around.

Thoughts

Your thoughts will betray you but your feeling never will. To explain this a little further the mind is a thinking mechanism with no feelings. It only has the ability to rationalize based on programmed information stored in memory. Where feeling have the ability to reach beyond the 3 dimensional reality and into other dimensions to gather information and advise you of pending trouble or advantageous situations that have not yet occurred. Your thoughts are seemingly good and secure but when it comes to a tight situation the mind tries to go to a safe place where it feels it is protecting you. However, in reality it is only drawing on old memories and solutions that may not be effective in a new situation. There are two ways to look at the phrase "your thoughts will betray you" one is to say your thoughts will reveal your intentions to others thus giving away your actions to others so they may prepare a defense or work against you in some manner. The second way you should see this phrase is where your thoughts will let you down in a time of need and convince you to take a wrong action or make a wrong choice at the wrong time that will defeat you and your true actions and beliefs.

On the flip side of the mind is the feeling center, this will not mislead you or lead you astray in the manner the mind can. The feelings are the reality of the matter at hand and should always be followed to make the better judgment in the situation at hand. The feelings are the same as the intuition we see so often in the feminine side found mostly in the female half of humanity. The male half has the same ability as the female but we have dumbed this down in the male side at this point in time. This is something that must be recultivated in order to evolve.

Multi dimensional thinking

When a light worker begins the transformation from a 3D human to a multidimensional, human the old usual thought patterns will start to change. This multidimensional thinking can be quite disconcerting at times. The transformation can cause forgetfulness, confusion, spaciness, and disorientation from time to time. The more one traverses into the new energy human the more often and with more frequent occurrences this can be noticed, it can even become a daily way of life to even forget what one just said or did moments before and one will have a difficult time to remember those moments. Long-term memory can be affected but usually not very much. All this is required when one moves from the old 3D way of thinking to a new energy level of much higher vibrational thinking patters. This will be the new multidimensional frequency of the new energy of earth and our surrounding universe. If one were to hold onto the old ways of thinking it would cause a greater time frame for the transformation to take place. Letting go of the old will be the fastest and more efficient way of the change.

The journey of a true lightworker

Question: what is the one answer that best sums up the lightworker's journey?

Answer: most would likely say BLISS however that would be wrong as the journey is an undertaking of the dark night of the soul which is a journey of TURMOIL in the beginning and most of the way through, it gets better near the end when the individual reaches the state of enlightenment one starts to experiences the road to be BLISSFUL. The transition from the human to the divine is a process of releasing all old concepts and past life ancestral incarnations. One must set them free before one can become free to be the divine human one desires to be. This can be an easy journey or it can be quite hard, it all depends on how well one can release the old story.

Chapter Seven

Future lifestyle

What will be the norm when humans are away from the era of money, control, and greed? Well, there is much that can and will come about without the use of money and it will come about far easier than the old era of restriction and red tape that we have read about so far. This old era did serve humanity in that it was a stepping-stone on the cosmic time clock. People of the future will view and live differently in some ways than those in the money era did. I wish to explain some possibilities that are more likely than others based on the probability of things that are due to a changing consciousness of the children who are now coming to earth.

Marriage & relationships

Relationships will no longer be out of neediness for financial security. People will not marry for money, as so many have. Instead they will marry for actual love of the other person. I don't mean to say people did not marry for love~ many did, but in the future money will not be a consideration at all in marriages. There will of course still be the physical and chemical attractions between people that initially draw them together, but the marriage will result from two people who are mutually in love with each other.

How does love actually work? Love is a rather complicated system, but I will try to explain some of it here.

Love, what is it?

Love is a mirror from one person to another, once we get past the pheromone stage of attraction. When we see and feel compatible qualities in another person that we like, it has the effect of drawing us to them and mirroring our own feelings and ideas of what love is back to us. We tend to love those that have that ability and desire to mirror back to us those feelings and ideas of what love is to each of us. Love is an emotion that works separately from the mind. Because of this one can feel love for another while simultaneously not liking the other's personality at all.

Put another way, we tend to send our feelings to others that we feel will return those same feelings. This is actually a mirroring of what we feel love is to ourselves; we send this out to someone that mirrors this back to us in a way we feel comfortable with. We then feel love for that other person. The actuality of this is that the love felt is really one's own love coming back via the mirroring effect. When both people do the same for each other, we then have a successful relationship with a continuous energy connection and exchange. The trigger for this is usually the physical and chemical attraction factors between people.

To recap a little: we do this only with others that we feel possess the qualities that would be most compatible with our own feelings and perceptions of what love is. Our senses reach out and tell us which people are most compatible and then we are strongly drawn to them. However, nobody ever thinks of it this way.

Two people can love each other but dislike each other's personalities. This can explain the phrase, "I love my spouse, but I can't stand him/her," as well as the phrase, "You don't know what you've got till it's gone."

What this is saying is there are two levels of communication going on between the two people. One is on the emotional level of heart to heart, which feels the actual love, and the other is on a personality and intellectual level, which finds faults and then dislikes the other person for their faults. When this happens, two people drive themselves apart. When they part, they miss the heart to heart connection that had been lost. So here we have an explanation of "You don't know what you've got till it's gone."

People of the future will live more from their heart level, making separation far less of a probability than it was in the old era. On the flip side of this we find that money is the driving force behind most all divorces.

In the future people will find themselves far more capable of making a compatible love transfer with many more people than in the money era, because they will understand the relationship of all things to the origination of the universe. In other words they will have a much higher understanding of themselves, love and of other people.

The point here is that you only feel your own love coming back to you from the other person. That is why it feels so good. It is your concept and feeling of love as you wish them to be. There is also some love that is what I call *distorted love*. It is when one person sends out love, but the other person sends only part of it back or they send an altered version of the original signal. This kind of love can lead to a marriage, but there will likely be conflict and or separation down the road (without even adding in the money factor) due to the distortions.

An outcome of relationships or even just two different people should also be mentioned here. When two people come together they create a whole different person as a whole. Mixing people in a relationship, or even friends, is like mixing chemicals. When you have two separate people and each one is a certain way all by themselves, mixing these people then creates a third person or even two other people that are different from who the original two people were all by themselves. This combining also creates a third compound or a third person out of the two. Like mixing two chemicals you will get a third very different compound. We can see this all the time in everyday relationships and friendships. Some of today's relationships, whether between a man and woman or business partners, can be quite volatile, especially when you add money (or maybe when you take it away). Some chemicals just do not mix well, and some are explosive when mixed together and some should never be mixed at all. When we take away the money factor in the future, we are in a sense removing the primer from the bomb and it will never go off.

A person may act one way with his or her friends but when he/she is with his or her partner, they act quite differently. Many young people have been accused by their old friends of changing so much after they meet a new mate that they are no longer the same friend they once were. They are accused of this on a regular basis. We could call this a chemical reaction of sorts that is done on more of an emotional level.

Marriage will be somewhat different in the future generations. It will be for love as we already know, but it will be for a time that may be shorter than the entire life span of each person that joins with another. We can see this today a great deal, but today it is called divorce and can be quite painful and messy because people do not understand the description of love as written above. In future times respect for the other person and a better understanding of the self will greatly curtail the hurt feelings of separation. People will move apart in agreement with each other with an understanding that each may need new experiences to properly evolve the soul that may not be available if they were to stay together. Future marriages will not have the licenses or contracts we have today between people, nor will they include the State as a third party to the union. Instead marriage will consist of two people being together for the time that they wish to stay together. Many will last all through the life of the two people and many will not. A traditional ceremony may be performed for celebration purposes, but not for any kind of legal entanglement as it has occurred up to the 20th century. I am not saying that marriage will last longer in the future--that may well be the case, but people will still change and some will move apart because of differing views and attitudes that develop over time out of the needs of the soul to evolve.

People of the 20th century do not realize that their marriage is a contract with the State giving permission for and control over the marriage. This three-way contract consists of the man the woman and the State. The license obtained from the State introduces control from a third party that can and does dictate the lives of those getting married through a contract known a marriage license. Why would anyone ever want such a situation? Future marriages will be far freer and more open compared to today.

Products

I have explained in prior chapters about cars and transportation means of the future with antigravity and different propulsion technologies. But there will be more advances than these. It is expected that since propulsion and antigravity will be different, there will also be differing needs for gravity and friction. Cars may run on low friction tires since there may be less need for them to stop a vehicle. The propulsion unit may well do most or even all the stopping. At the time this book is written, it is not expected that cars will yet be flying or hovercraft types. And it is not likely they will see the scattering of molecules for transport yet to be invented. There will be frictionless bearings—maybe a super bearing that will be invented that will never wear out. Propulsion may well go in a different direction of magnetics and antigravity, in which case the tires may become a super friction type, quite the opposite of the low friction tires mentioned, or it may be a combination of both. The car may be as light as a feather from the antigravity unit on board but the tires may be super heavy gravity grabbers that stick to the ground extremely well. This car would stop very easily because the car being very light would have little or no inertia from the car body to stop. Magnetics is a field our scientists of today are just starting to scratch the surface of. This future magnetic technology may result in a motor that produces horsepower like a gas motor with rotating shafts and will be housed in a self-contained unit that will be capable of producing hundreds of horsepower from a relatively lightweight unit of a rather small dimensional size (about one third the size of a six cylinder gas motor of the 20th century). It will not use any fossil fuels. But it may go the way of the earlier mentioned transducer style of propulsion. The probabilities are always open to new paths.

Tracking devices will be used in cars as a signature signal of the unit if it gets misplaced or lost, or if there is suspicion of trouble with the unit or the occupant. This will be used when no communication can be obtained from the occupant on their personal device.

Communications will be far more advanced than they are now to the point where all communications will be carried on the person in the form of a small microchip in a wristwatch style or a type of pocket unit that is easy to carry. This device will have the voice capability to talk back to the person and it can store and communicate with all world databases to retrieve any information instantly. It is likely that this unit will have an organic living memory cell as its processor. Currently the governments of the world are planning a new tracking and control device. This Motorola tracking chip that is being produced in the late 20th century will be scrapped, as people will not accept them in the near future. The issuance of these chips on the population is planned in a way that will be in direct relation to a world money situation, where the system is still using money, but it will be more like credits. There will be no paper money. The plan is to do away with paper money and inject a rice size micro chip under the skin of the back side of the right hand of people for two reasons: one will be for tracking purposes and the other will be to access your bank account and everything about the person with the chip. You will scan your hand when you buy something and it will be deducted from your credits that you have earned from your job. Your labor is considered the wealth of the government. This chip will also kill the person if they attempt to remove it, tampering will cause it to rupture and inject a deadly poison into the blood. There is a huge stockpile of these chips somewhere in Asia at this time. The plan is to start using these chips in what are called third world countries. The people there are not as sophisticated, nor are they as educated as the people of most other countries, so they expect no resistance to the implanting of the chips. It is also expected that they will implant millions of people without their consent or knowledge, possibly through a vaccine shot that will be created from a manufactured epidemic of some sort.

Back to transportation, trains will also use the same technology as cars and trucks; however, it will be a novelty to ride them just for the fun of it and not so much for travel, because planes will be considered 100% safe for travel with the use of these antigravity enhancements. They will still have wings but will use no fuels as they do in the 20th century. They will be wider and longer with far more comfort and room for the passengers. They will take off and land in a far shorter distance than the planes of today.

Recreational vehicles will be used far more in the future due to the changing life styles that will emerge. Many more people will live in RVs and travel all around the country and even the world. Mobility will be popular during this time period. People will want to see the world they live on rather than just read about it in books and watch movies of other people's travels. Experiencing different cultures will also be a great teaching and evolutionary tool for all people.

Power and appliances

Soon after the development of a self-contained power supply for homes is made available, power units for smaller appliances will become available as well. Even the smallest appliances will employ small magnetic water or light sources of self-contained power to run them. They will not require a cord for external electricity. They could run on a magnetic motor for the moving parts, and an energy cell for the non-moving parts. They may, however, be run totally on a power cell similar to the batteries we use today, but these cells will never deplete themselves and will last longer than the appliance itself.

Even before this development, the energy stored in water will be discovered and developed by scientists to power cities all over the world. When the future scientists discover this power, they will be able to power the largest cities for three years from just one cubic centimeter of water. Crystals are another form of energy that can already be seen in today's lasers; this, too, will be further developed into energy sources. Perhaps a crystal will be the heart of the small appliance power source. Yet another source of inexhaustible energy is the matter between molecules that is known as the *all that is*. This energy will be discovered and harnessed in the far distant future. As we evolve new inventions will flood into our reality of earth from the sources of that which has all the creation abilities we as humans still lack.

Cooking in the future will be somewhat different. We see today the advanced use of microwaves and light for preparing foods. Microwaves are efficient but destroy some of the nutrients in the food and are thus less healthy for the body when eaten. The halogen light cooking devices are better for cooking, they take a bit longer to cook but still are far less time consuming than cooking by fire. They are generally less messy and require less energy. Sound can also be developed to vibrate molecules of the moisture found in all things to heat or cook foods.

Climate controls in cars, homes, planes, etc. will operate by means of light and sound waves combined to almost instantly adjust the temperature and humidity for comfort in a zone without the need to force air through a cooling unit. These units will even be used outdoors for spaces as small as a picnic or as large as a stadium.

Entertainment will change as well. The popular violent movies of the money era will be like us today watching some of the very old movies from the twenties where the physical movements were too fast and jerky and had no sound. The new entertainment will be of a nature that is relevant to the evolutionary state of the mind. This means that there will still be many different types of movies and plays, but any violence used will likely only be in comedies. Action adventures will still be popular.

Punishment--this will be a thing of the past and most definitely forgotten and added only to our museums and history books. You should already understand this topic from the first part of this book.

Education will not be limited in any way. All things required to live on earth will be taught and they will treat young people with the intelligence they deserve. In the term *all things*, it is meant that a better overall rounding of subjects as a base for life will be taught in all levels of school, then as the student desires more or unique types of understanding, that, too, will be available right in the everyday classrooms at any age the student desires it. The education of the future will be designed to give the student the understanding one needs to live in the world. Today we only teach basic history, math, reading, and writing. Many of the students will know far more than the teachers due to the advanced understanding a child brings from past evolutions. We have always seen this in each new generation that understands more than their parents did. But it will get even more noticeable in future generations. The future generation will be so advanced at birth they will be able to read and write before they can walk.

This bears repeating, the children from the beginning will be more advanced than the teachers just the same as we were more advanced than our parents. Remember the falling object theory of speed to understand how this will be even greater in times ahead. The new children of the future will be able to see colors that we today cannot. Their thought patterns will measure very differently than ours do today. Different thought patterns mean different ways of thinking, which will lead to the changes in the entire world and the elimination of the oppressive systems of the 20th century. It has already begun. If you think about the writings in this book, at least one such child/man who is now an adult is writing about the changes that are upon us and the changes to come in the very near future.

Houses will be fully self-contained for all climates, even if the occupants are away for long periods of time, they will control the heat as needed in cold seasons and let fresh air in during warm seasons, all without the need of human initiation if desired. The lawns will water much as they do today, but with added features such as a self-draining irrigation system so it will not freeze in colder weather. The watering may be from the roots by means of mesh type inlay under the sod rather than from blowing water over the top of the grass. The current method is inefficient and wastes too much with the current availability of water in so many heavily populated areas.

NASA will still be around, as a desire to travel outside our planet's atmosphere will be heightened in the people of the new era. There will be much advancement in technology, even greater than today's developments by NASA. However, the NASA of the future will be a world joint venturing into space and technology. Many of the smartest minds will gravitate to the many NASA labs that will be located around the globe. The name may change because we will have a smaller government as discussed earlier. But technology will go on in a big way. There will also be other labs started by people that want to do their own thing with technology. Many will want to see the earth from space and trips will be available for all who wish to go as far as the moon just to look back at the marvelous globe of mother Gaia (earth).

All this will happen due to the advanced understanding of all people all over the world. Drawing on part one of this book, there will be a far greater ease of life in comparison to the past eras. People all over the earth will treat total strangers as dear old friends they have known all their lives.

Ms. Alison:

Good morning class how is everyone today? Please slip your memory chips into your desk stations and we will talk about the two chapters you read last night.

Let me start by saying you have all done well so far for the very beginning of the year. I am pleased at the concentration levels I see in all of you. Did you know that in some of the schools in the past the schools had to have police patrol the halls due to the guns and drugs that the students would bring to school? It became so bad that almost all schools hade some kind of patrol or security. At times there were shootings by students of other students and teachers. During the later part of the money era, the students were not interested in their own growth, rather they were more interested in partying and making trouble in a rebellious way. This was caused directly from the money mentality of the society as a whole. Parents had to work long hours, which caused problems in the family unit where attention was needed but could not be given by the parents. Many of the stresses were passed on to the children by the system and the parents that struggled with money issues. As the children learned of their society in this negative way they became very uncomfortable and even hateful and rebellious of their surroundings. Many students were not recognized as being different in a good way, but rather they were seen as troublemakers. What the schools did not see was that a child may have been an Indigo child and as such needed to be treated differently than a non-indigo child.

The lack of recognition is most likely what caused much of the violence in the child. It must have been extremely frustrating to the child to be so different and know it. But they were in a world that could not see or understand what they understood. Sometimes violence would result from a misunderstood Indigo child and the treatment he/she got from parents, schools, and friends. Stealing and fighting was a very big thing among students from the age of ten and up. The system then would punish those they thought were different instead of sitting down with them and trying to understand there needs. All of you today would be considered far more advanced than the indigos of the past. We also recognize you and those that we know are different than you are and we do our best to help them along in our society so they do not get lost.

Well, let's start with Sharon today.

Sharon:
Yes, Ms. Alison.

That little story makes us sound like angels.

[Snickering in the room.]

Ms. Alison:
Sharon, compared to then, you are angels. In fact, you would be surprised at just how right you really are in that regard.

Please, Sharon, give us your impression of the first section on chapter six, *Evolution of the Soul*.

Sharon:
After reading this it seems that the corrupt system of government, and especially the banks, planned to and did re-enslave the people much like or even worse than the black slaves in the deep South of our country we read about two years ago. Only this time they did it without firing a shot or using any physical force to chain the people and make them work for them again. The people unwittingly walked right into this trap and didn't even know they were slaves again—only this time to money. This time it was far bigger than the phenomenon of slavery of blacks from the South; this time it was the entire country. This is what the War Between the States and the Boston Tea Party were fought to end, yet this says that they were right back where they started from, only they didn't even know it this time.

We are sovereigns, aren't we?

Ms. Alison:
Yes, Sharon, today we are but it is not important to be one now because we have no laws to control us like they had, so it doesn't matter if we are or not. Please continue on with the rest.

Sharon:
Okay. It seems that some of the people of the later part of this era found out about the deceptions and were trying to combat them and even found a way to become sovereign again. That sounds a lot like freeing slaves, I think. The book goes on to talk about our evolution and past life regressions. When I read about this part, Alice and I decided we wanted to go and do a past life regression this weekend and see what we could remember from our past.

Ms. Alison:
Sharon, that seems like a good idea you will have to tell us about that next week.

Sharon:
We will. Now, the next thing I remember is that evolution never goes backwards, it can only go forward, but it also only exists in the current moment. I somehow understand this because we can think of things we have experienced in the past, but we cannot think of things in our future because they have not been experienced yet. We can only think of things we would like to happen, but not as if they have actually come to pass, such as plans we make or would like to make. I also understand the potentials of what may happen as a set of variables based on the present circumstances. Like right now, we are all at school and later we will all go home. We may think of different ways we would take to get home, which could include many different ways, but only one of them will ultimately become the actual experience of getting home. I am thinking of riding with Alice, but that may not be the actual way I will get home, because she may want to go do something else that I will not choose to go do with her. So we have the understandable variables of possibility. This is for the short term, I know, but it is the same for the long term as well. At least this is how I understand this potential as it was written about in this book.

We do however have the multidimensional ability to use our feelings to further feel out the most probable outcome of something in our futures. We as humans are still learning as we evolve into our futures about this developing tool.

From our sensibility classes we have learned the seven-second rule of creation. As I understand this rule, when we hold a thought from five to seven seconds straight with clear intent, that idea or thought will manifest in reality in the physical world. I can remember doing this several times in my life. For example, when I liked Jimmy Drang back in fourth grade, but he didn't like me or even any other girls, I used that technique. My mother told me of this rule I guess just to comfort me because I was upset about him so much, so I used that rule and about a month later he asked me to walk home with him. Then I used it again when I was fourteen to be more popular with some of the other kids in school. Later that semester I was voted the top of the class for the overall academic student of the year. And the next year, all the really cool kids became my friends and they still are. Maybe I shouldn't say that because it sounds like segregation among friends and I do not want anyone to think I don't like them, because I do. I love school and all my friends very much. It's just that back then I was a little insecure and wanted to be better liked because I thought it would help boost my own self-esteem. As I look back, I see that it really did. So the seven-second rule does work and it has helped me a lot. By holding a thought for seven seconds straight our feeling centers are able to connect to the thought and manifest it for us.

Ms. Alison:
Thank you, Sharon. That is a great point. I want to add the saying *Be mindful of your thoughts*. This phrase is really quite accurate, as we have seen from Sharon's explanation. I want to take this a little further so we all understand that it can work in negative ways too. While dwelling on a problem one has, one may well be making the problem worse because one is dwelling on the problem itself. Instead, the person should be dwelling on the solution or resolution of the problem in one's life in order to see the problem as resolved or removed from one's life. But as Sharon used the seven-second rule, she was creating something she wanted that was not a part of her life yet. This is a positive use of this tool.

Sharon, please continue with the rest of this section.

Sharon:
Okay, Ms. Alison. Next he talks about remembering past lives on a regular basis. I think he is right about us being much less evolved than we would be if we could remember all the past things and ways we lived. If we did remember and think like we did in past lives, maybe we would still be living like some of the cavemen did.

Allan:
Hey, Sharon, how's your dinosaur pee water taste?

Sharon:
Very funny, Allan.

Ms. Alison:
Okay, Allan, Sharon has the floor.

Allan:
Yes, ma'am.

Sharon:
Thank you, Ms. Alison. The next thing I remember is the latter part of this era where people were taking and stealing and abusing most all others for money.

Ms. Alison:
Yes, Sharon, this is accurate. But not all people did this. It was done by many but not all. Remember, we did make it through that era alive. Go on, Sharon.

Sharon:
Well, from this section the accomplishment thing was something that really hindered people back then in a big way. If one person was unlucky or unskilled in some way, they would not get the money that it would take to have a better way of life as one would like to have. This was a really screwed up time from all this money that caused so many problems for the entire world. The stress of this must have been unbearable at times.

Ms. Alison:
Yes, Sharon, it was. But you also must remember they got themselves into this slowly so they had a great deal of time to become used to the pressures. They just did not see the big picture of all that they had created for themselves and all the ill effects that came from the use of this money.

Go on, Sharon...

Sharon:
He did understand the truer meaning of peace from the way he described it. I think that is the way we understand it today too. I feel that he is talking directly to us in this class as he talks about the future students. It seems as if he can see us while he is writing this book back than.

Ms. Alison:
Sharon, maybe he could or at least envision us in some way.

Sharon:
Like the comment Allan made about the water, I did not get mad at him. I know he was only playing and I understand that the water may very well have

been dinosaur pee at some time, but today the earth has cleaned it many times over since then. I would never get mad at anybody over such a statement, not even for something that was directed to hurt me in some way. I understand that sometimes people get into a bad way of behaving for many reasons and they will say or do things they would not ordinarily do, so I do not get mad at them for isolated incidents. I am confident within myself and I know who I am so even intended hurtful things generally do not bother me.

He also spoke about time speeding up in that time period. I don't know about then, so I cannot give any good comments on the differences between the times of then and now. I guess that the last part of this section did happen, as we are here today so those people must have made some positive changes in their thinking way back then.

Ms. Alison:
Thank you, Sharon that was good. And, yes, they did make some changes for the better that this author is not likely to be aware of in his time because those changes came some time later, but they were much like what he wrote about here.

There were several sections to this reading assignment. Let's ask Peter to do this next section.

Peter:
Okay, Ms. Alison. The thing that I remember first is the stepping-stone part where he says that we, the future generations, will use this in future times as well. But I see that in their time they were also using there past struggles as stepping-stones for their current evolution, which leads to us in the now. He went on to talk about future probabilities—again which Sharon spoke of, so I guess that there is little point in going over that again. But I would like to comment on the marriage thing.

Ms. Alison:
Excuse me, Peter, since this next section goes into some detail, I want you to just give us highlights and comparisons of the differences between then and now.

Peter:
Okay, Ms. Alison. Back then marriage was considered a must from what I

have read, and it came with a contract, but today it is more like what he said it would be for the most part. My parents, for example, are not married like they were back then. My parents did a celebration in the beginning and they do one again every ten years to celebrate because they are happy with each other. I also have read about all the divorce they used to have and my parents and friends' parents have never shown me any signs of separating. It seems to me that we have more harmonious relationships with each other today than they did back then. I have seen some people move away from each other today, but I think it is far less common than it was back then.

For the products section and cars: I do not drive. I just get in the car and tell it where I want it to take me. I have not been interested in what's under the hood. I have not tried to drive it myself yet, but I plan to when I get my own car. Right now, I am too afraid of messing up dad's car. So from reading what he wrote back then, I guess he was close in a general sense of description about how cars would work today like Candy said earlier.

The trains are pretty much the same as the cars, I think. But I have seen those old trains at the open range wild animal park that spew all that smoke. They are neat, but they really create a lot of smoke and noise. We have an RV too. Looking at the history catalogs in the library shows that they used to drive theirs back then. We just get in and plan a trip and it takes us there and then back again. Ours is like a house when we get to a parking station for RVs. Dad pushes a button and both sides move out all the way from the front to the rear. It's almost as big as our house on the east side wing. But while we are traveling, it's kind of cramped. The pictures of the antiques I have seen were sometimes only about seven foot wide with some parts that would slide out when they parked them, which made them a little bit bigger inside. I like ours because it has everything we have from home and I can seal off the back so my parents don't even know I am there. I can lower the temperature just the way I like it or even freeze my sister out; and I can watch or do whatever I want while they are playing cards during the trip on the road.

Ms. Alison:
Okay, you are wandering now. Back to the class, Peter.

Peter:
Okay, Ms. Alison. The next part I remember is the punishment section. He didn't say much about this in this section because it was covered earlier, but I am glad we don't do what he described they did back then to people now.

The education part is pretty accurate for today, because I have always been able to find anything I wanted about history, mechanical subjects, art, music and everything else just by asking the world net through my information unit. I just ask my communication information devices, like the one in Sam's old watch, about what I want to know (I call mine chip, because they're so small) and it returns the information with pictures and sometimes sounds that go with the topics. It has never told me it couldn't find anything that I have asked it to get. We sometimes watch the old movies from that era, but my mom says some of them are not too good to watch, but I have called some of them up anyway to see what they were all about. I don't like the killing stuff too much—that's no way to treat another person. But I do like the old cars when they crash; those are really cool to watch.

I don't know too much about that old NASA stuff because I am not a scientist or mechanical type, but we are scheduled to go on vacation next winter for an outer space trip I am looking forward to that. They still call it NASA sometimes. We do have a lot of advancements in power usage, travel, cooking, communications, and comforts for home and a whole lot more that I can't remember and far too many to go into listing for the class. I guess that's it for this section, Ms. Alison.

Ms. Alison:
Thank you, Peter.

Francis can you take the section on the new earth?

Francis:
Yes ms. Alison, this is something we are all taught about from early childhood. I agree about what he says and what we understand today about this gaseous form in space. We can see this with telescopes and it does look like he describes. Some of us can communicate with the beings from this planet. They teach us the way of harmony and allowing others to be who they are. There is not much more to say about this planet except that the physical earth is evolving to a state of existence more like the new earth is.

Ms. Alison:
Since that was a short section can you also take the next two sections on beliefs and travel?

Francis:
Yes, the beliefs section is all about what we believe at a core level is what we in turn create in our physical reality. I agree from my own experience that taking another's beliefs can be a mistake because what one believes may be right for them but not so right for me as I am not on the same path as that other person may be on. In general we as a whole of humanity believe in similar ways of existence and our progressing into the future.

Where he talks about travel he is mostly talking about travel throughout the universe in our sleep states. For me I have traveled to many distant places and I understand that these places are in part some of the planets I have incarnated on in other lives. Some of the dreams I have are a teaching to help me release those old life times. I sometimes see things I do not understand but I am sure they have a meaning and reason for coming as they do. We understand that these nights of dreams or should I say travel often leave us drained in the morning, feeling more tired than when we went to sleep the night before.

Ms. Alison:
We need a fresh voice to take the next topic. Lets say Tammy, are you up to the challenge on spiritual groups?

Tammy:
Yes Ms. Alison
This is a topic of human emotions. He seems to be talking about the 20th Century humans with all the pressures they had to endure. It seems to me that it was a difficult matter to let go of the ingrained emotional issues that the society unsuspectingly taught through all the problems they had to deal with. Of course it all stemmed from the money mentality he spoke of earlier. The author was not immune to these emotions either and he admitted he gets his buttons pushed at time. We still have our buttons to deal with but ours are far less than theirs were because we do not have to deal with the oppression and control issues they had to live under constantly. The thing there were doing was getting back on course as he put it and that has lead us a race of people to where we are today and that is the important thing in that section.

Ms. Alison:
Tammy please go ahead and do the next part about disconnecting.

Tammy:
Ok, this sections explains itself better than I can but what I got from it is to live in a system of mass consciousness that is not evolving as it should one had to disconnect from that conscious awareness in order to move up in a vibrational state of being. We know we have to increase our vibrational states to be able to evolve. This is because the refined realms we are headed for are already vibrating at a higher frequency than we are now. Our lower vibrations cannot exist in the higher vibrations; we would burst into flames or disintegrate if we suddenly found ourselves in the higher vibrations. The frequencies are just too different to be able to move into that vibration. We do know that higher frequency beings can manifest in our vibration for a time but we cannot go to theirs.

To get back to the disconnect he talked about I can see how it must have been hard at times to make the separation with all that was being passed around from all those that were not evolving but merely living through the struggles of daily life under those conditions. Today we have a light sense about our mass consciousness all around the world that is conducive to evolution of the self that is far greater than back then.

Ms. Alison:
Thank you Tammy. Lets see, who have we not heard from yet? Sylvia would you give us your rendition on the Your Story section?

Sylvia:
I would be glad to Ms. Alison.

I need to say the same thing Tammy said, this section speaks for itself better than I can. My take on this is that I understand what he is saying and I am of course doing this I my life today as so many of us are doing who are on the path of ascension. I have found that I tend to hold onto my past life stories that have become comfortable in this life even for my young age. We see today that this is directly related to our travels in our dreams and that it is contained in out DNA as he stated. You would think that today we would no longer have these old life times hanging around but we do. Many if not most of us were not likely to have been on earth in the 20th Century. We have come in now with all our old baggage still intact, it's just that we have come in at a time on earth when evolution is a mainstream way of life so for us it is easier. There was some talk about Karma in this section but I think that is better explained later in other sections so we should leave that for then.

Ms. Alison:
Yes Sylvia I agree that is a good idea. Sylvia please do the next two sections on Feelings and Thought.

Sylvia:
Well ok, this section is about knowing or feeling what you know in your heart. I think most of us can distinguish from thinking and feeling but I must speak mostly for myself. I do see the difference but they must have had a harder time when it came to this important difference. Otherwise he would not have written about this in this book. This is similar to the seven-second rule but it is done with conscious intent to know what you want to occur in the deepest levels of the soul and heart. From my understanding of all this, this is the direct connection to the higher self that is not housed in the physical form. This higher self directs the life as it is necessary but when it gets signals from the physical for a need or desire it will work them in to manifest that which is asked for into the physical. Thoughts are never transmitted to the higher self. You can scream all you want but the higher self will never hear your demands. In our house evolution is talked about from time to time to see who is doing what. My dad says when he was young he tried to make something happen by thinking about it really hard and throwing a tantrum with his mother but no matter what he did he could not make it happen. He thought he had succeeded but it came back time after time in a matter of months or maybe a year down the road. Later in his teen years he understood what he was doing and learned how to transfer thought. He said he was still unsure about some things until he met mom and they worked on his understanding more. In a few weeks he was able to move his thoughts and release a bad nightmare that was haunting him all through childhood. So thought can, not only deceive you but also trick you into thinking you have had a success when you really have not.

Ms. Alison:
Thank you Sylvia. Class we are going to skip the next two very short sections on multidimensional thinking and the journey of a light-worker because we already know what they are and that we are already on that path.

Ms. Alison:
If you have read ahead you know that the next chapter is where the author changes gears even more and moves toward a higher internal human direction where he explains more of the issues of their time and the requirements for making a change in consciousness. He starts this out in a way I did not think

he would because it seems he is referring to the earlier chapters about government by saying this next sentence. Quote: *The world's systems of control need to be scrapped and a whole new one started with peace and love between all people.*

Okay, class, I will go ahead and read this chapter to the class.
[Ms. Alison reads from the book.]

Chapter Eight

The higher understandings and aspects of the coming times just ahead

I wish to first give some explanations as a basis for this chapter.

This universe system is being transformed from an old energy system to a new energy system because of the evolution and uplifting of human consciousness. As humans, we are growing and learning all the time. This is becoming an exponential learning situation. The more we learn, the faster we learn, and the faster we evolve. Evolution is a vibrational increase in our physical and mental makeup. This occurs in several areas of life from our basic needs to a spiritual understanding of the self. The new energy is one of self-governance by each individual to live as one chooses in harmlessness with all others.

The system does not see this coming and will die a hard death due to ignorance and refusal to believe their time is over. There is nothing they can do about it. After all, how long has any governance ever lasted in our known history? Rome was the longest known existing democracy, but it vanished in the blink of an eye in comparison to the age of the planet herself and all the prior civilizations that came long before our current known history. The people of the money era for whom this book was written will not see this change in their lives. It will come as the generations of the old energy die off and the new babies come in with the advanced understandings of truth. The ones coming now with this understanding are called Indigo children. But at the same time *our* understandings are the first steps out of a dying era into this new era. We carry the genetics of creation that the newborns will use as their genetic building blocks from our DNA that carries the coding of our past generations and understanding into the next level of existence. More on the Indigos in later.

Karma

Here is another concept that is little known to the system of law and control, and to most other people for that matter. First, karma that a person accrues can be good karma or bad karma. Bad Karma is incurred anytime a person interferes with another person's evolution in physical form; when a person goes against the free will of another person by forcing one's will upon another. What this means is that everybody alive has come to earth in the physical form to go through experiences that were setup by one's higher self, and these are directed in part by the subconscious. One then gains an understanding of what is needed. One is then directed based on the higher self's requirements for the soul to evolve. There is only a small part of the soul and higher self housed in the physical body, the rest is in a higher level of existence. It is close by but not in the physical reality. You could say it is next door in another dimensional reality watching and directing what it sees to be required for the individual. The higher self does use the system to teach oneself the required lessons at this time. This is because we may need some hard lessons at times to get out of our ruts. It is hard to know when new karma is being created and when old karma is being settled. I will not go into any intricacies here on this subject, as they are very complicated. So complicated that the human mind could not fully comprehend their workings. I will say that karma was created and is used by humans, it was not created by the *all that is*. This is something that we created over time as a checks and balances system for both right and wrong and to keep the human in balance for their own evolution purposes.

This is only a small part of how we evolve to the next level. First there is no good or bad right or wrong. Good karma that which we like to experience is accrued when a person does a kindness to another person. Negative karma that is due has to be balanced at some time, whether it is in the current life or a future life in order for anyone to evolve. Let's say, for example, a cop or a judge makes an unjust or harsh judgment on a person. That judge or cop has just created negative karma with the person they did the injustice to. Or they may be settling a past karma. In this case to know whether a settlement is actually taking place. A release will be felt by the one being judged after the situation is over. If not, a frustration may be the experience by the one being judged for some time to come after the situation passes. This frustration is the sub-conscience telling you that this situation is out of balance. New karma has been created.

Another thing to remember here is that one may create karma that another can join. Such as when a cop gives a ticket and then the judge picks up on the cop's ticket and fines the person that got the ticket. This is one way karma is created—and now there are two people that have to repay or balance the karma incurred to the person they made the karma with. In many cases the karma will not be balanced until another lifetime when both parties are unaware of the prior life's debts.

At that time people may be in reverse rolls and then do the same thing to each other in reverse to balance the karma. It may, however, be settled in the current life in many other ways, depending on the higher self's direction and on whether it is deemed to be necessary to have an interaction with the same two souls again or whether it can be settled through hardship of another kind for the one who incurred the negative karma. With the compression of time as we feel it today karma is being settled more often in the same life and the settlement of karma is coming quickly. (A song comes to mind: *Instant Karma* by John Lennon.) Today we have all felt at times that it seems there just aren't enough hours in a day as there used to be. This is due to time compression and planetary evolution. The planet evolves too. Think of it this way: the planet is the mother of everything alive on it. Our bodies came from the minerals of the planet and will go back to it when we leave. Only our experiences and consciousness will be taken with us when we leave. Our evolution is a steady change in vibration to a higher frequency. As the vibrations increase, the time will compress even further. At the time this book is being written, our days are four hours shorter than they were in the early 1980's

I have used the legal system, as an example above because I see how much karma is generated everyday by that system. There is karma being generated all over by all sorts of people daily, both good karma and bad. The good karma is what we want to get back as it is always pleasant. Karma can be paid back anywhere from 10- to 100-fold more than the original karma that was incurred by the victim that will now be experienced by the perpetrators of the karma. As mentioned earlier, sometimes the karma will be repaid in the current life through hardship experienced by the perpetrator of the karma, either good (pleasant) or (bad). The hardship can be sickness, financial hardship, or a loss of something that would be disappointing or devastating to the person balancing the debt. The level of repayment is based on the original karma perpetrated on a victim that kept that person from evolving in the normal course that it would have naturally taken. The multiplying comes in when the karma held the victim of the karma back where it would not have if the incident had not happened. The interference that was done also holds all parties back from their normal course of evolution as planned by the higher self until the karma is balanced.

You may be saying, "Why?" or "How could this be so?" It is because earth is a planet that has free will. This means that anyone can do anything they please to anyone at any time. The karma throws the natural order and flow of things in relation to the earth out of balance and this must be rebalanced in order to move on. Personal Karma also holds the planet back from evolving as it normally would.

However, free will is rather like a test to see what you will do here on earth. Will you choose to do harm or will you live in harmlessness? As the religious texts all say, we should do unto others as we would have done unto us. This is a state of non-interference with another's free will and course of evolution. Another way to put this in today's language is to permit others their choices. All are on a path, but all are not on the same path. There are many paths to the higher levels but they all lead to the same place. Look at a road map and you will see there are many ways to get to a destination, some are very direct and some are very long and out of the way. What one person thinks or takes as their truth may not be appropriate for another, and all must allow all others their paths and beliefs. When the system says you cannot do something, the system has no right to interfere in what you do or believe. This would again be negative karma for the system. This can all get very complicated as I have already said, and dissecting this is really beyond the scope of this book.

Church

The church says you must live your life a certain way or you will not be able to get into heaven. They say things such as how it would be easier for a camel to pass thru the eye of a needle than it is for a rich man to get into heaven. This was misinterpreted and is being used to say to you that you should be humble to the church and give your wealth away, preferably to the church, and then you can get into heaven. I have said before that money is not something created by God. It was not needed for a person to be born nor is it needed when you die. Man created money and the churches require it because they are a business that exists in a 3-D world. Another one is "only through the son of God may you get to heaven." This is another way of saying if you do not do as *we say*, you will never get to heaven--as if they have some kind of monopoly on the Son of God that you do not have. This is a total lie.

All that is required is for a person to desire to be in heaven. It is not a physical place you know. It is a state of consciousness on a different vibrational level than earth is on. For people on earth, heaven is what you make of it in your mind and heart. The vibrations of heaven are far greater than we currently have on earth, but getting there is far easier than one may think. Ask and you will receive. Be sincere in your asking of the higher realms and you will be guided to the correct information and people that can show you the right way to experience heaven on earth right now, not after you die. Heaven exists simultaneously on earth right alongside your current consciousness. Take that step to the side and you will see and find heaven right now.

Change to put it simply
IF YOU KEEP DOING WHAT YOU'VE ALWAYS DONE YOU WILL KEEP GETTING WHAT YOU'VE ALWAYS GOTTEN

IF YOU WANT CHANGE, CHANGE WHAT YOU THINK, DO AND SAY AND CHANGE WILL MANIFEST IN YOUR LIFE AUTOMATICALLY
WE ARE NOT HUMANS TRYING TO HAVE A HIGHER EXPERIENCE WE ARE HIGHER BEINGS ALREADY HERE HAVING A HUMAN EXPERIENCE

Some public changes
In the public sector of things there will be some noticeable changes in the future in the ways things will alter themselves based on our current reality and perceptions. One way will be the way restaurants will interact with the general populace. They will be in business to serve others on a level that is far more personal than it is now; restaurants will have a caring attitude toward all others. Most restaurants will serve only healthy foods with a balanced nutritional menu; this includes fast food restaurants. Imagine McDonalds serving a nutritional and healthy hamburger, or maybe meat will be an oddity, as people will not want to kill animals so much for food. Meat *will* still be on our menus, as the animals know they are here in service to humanity to provide protein, dairy, and other goods. Animals know this instinctively and freely offer themselves in this service. These restaurants will become more of a romantic meeting spot for couples. Some restaurants will cater strictly to business meetings and offer a well-designed room for food and beverages as well as a comfortable atmosphere for dining and listening to the meetings at hand.

Anger

Anger is an emotion of great strength and force. Do we need it? *Yes*, we do. Anger that is run out of control is a bad thing and can cause some damage in physical and emotional areas of our lives. But on the flip side, anger has spurred us to do many things that have advanced our lives on personal and worldly levels.

Anger is a part of us that we cannot deny. It has a purpose. Early man drew on his anger along with hunting skills to hunt and kill for food. It was designed to help us out of our laziness and get us moving again when we needed it. Anger was built into us as a tool to keep others from walking all over us, and the free will within our soul. Anger has manifested very badly at times because we have found ourselves in wars, under oppression from people with power over us (especially in the current system) and separation from loved ones and more. The anger of oppression creates frustration that can at times drain our energy to the point of physical illness.

Anger is good for us in that it has helped us as a people to emerge from under conditions such as oppression from others, from bad situations in business and personal relationships, and it has helped us to break free from many things that were confining to the free soul. It has at times given us a balance between right and wrong. It has shown us after the fact that we should not go off like a bomb and cause damage to others either physically or emotionally. It has shown us that warring with others only leaves behind hurt and devastation of all peoples by our use of anger and force. Anger brings force. That force is sometimes good and sometimes bad, it is all in how it is used by the individual. We can force our will onto another and cause him harm, or we can force ourselves out of a situation that is threatening or potentially physically harmful to us. A balanced individual would use anger and force as a tool to protect himself from harm in one's life as needed, but would not intentionally use it to cause harm to others, as a war does.

Wars?

War is a great creator of force and anger and leaves a wide path of devastation wherever it goes. This kind of anger and force is created by politicians that are too scared to fight their own battles and recklessly go about creating hurt with other people and their country on a large scale. These politicians then call upon the people that they supposedly represent to go to other countries and kill the people of that country on behalf of the politician who created the war in the first place. So we the people fighting the wars are forced to kill other innocent individuals by force placed upon them from both of the government's stupidity and carelessness. The politicians will not go and fight over the anger and force they generated in others. We the people did not create it they did.

They then come and lay it on the people with a patriotic duty slogan that says it is your patriotic duty to defend your country from aggressors. The ironic part is that the aggressors are the politicians and the government that created the war in the first place. Why should you be forced to kill and be killed for their mistakes and carelessness?

Turn away and let them fight their own wars and problems and we will see them stop making those careless decisions and laying them in our laps. The people of both countries should tell their politicians to go, and fight, and be killed for their own mistakes. They will soon stop making trouble in other countries.

Peace

We do not live in a free society at all. We hear that this is a free country and we have freedom of speech. We are free because our troops fought for our freedom, etc. But who did we fight? We fought each other. People fought other people. All that is total bullshit. The world does not know what real freedom or peace really is. The world lives under constant oppression and control by others we know as laws and religious beliefs and even from our own minds because of what we choose to believe. Your own beliefs keep you in bondage to yourself and others based on what you have been taught, what you take as your own truth and then subsequently believe in.

What is real freedom you ask? It is the ability to walk the earth without a care in the world, to do as you please, to be self-governing, to know the true love from within and to be totally connected to your higher self and living as your true divine self in human form. For many that is a strong sentence, but it is the truth of what real peace really is. Freedom is not a lack of war or lack of oppression, that is just lack of war and or oppression. True peace comes from within and is radiated out into the world for all to see. It is contagious and when someone sees this true love and peace coming from within you, they then want to be near this energy or near you to take part in it. When a person is in that state, like a newborn baby, there is no hate, anger, oppression, control, etc. in those around them. You instead allow others to be themselves. You do not make or enforce laws to control others. You know and love all others as you know and love yourself, because you see the love, beauty and wonder in them that are also in you and in all of creation. In other words, you then see and respect the God that is in all. This is true peace.

As humans we really have no reason to fight with one another. There is only reason to live, as the original setup was designed for us. They call it the Garden of Eden in the religious texts.

It has been said that the governments of the world are going to make a very big mistake that they fail to see as the undoing of the systems. The impending marshal law that they are now planning against their own people may well cause their undoing. Chances are this statement will not happen because the system fears it own demise from retaliation of the people. Further oppression can only push the people and their souls so far before they will stand up and walk away from the whole mess. Today people do not care for or about others that they do not know. Many times you get a bad attitude from all sorts of people who are busy with their own problems due to the overall situation that is caused by control and the use of money.

We all need to turn away from this attitude and search within for a more reasonable and peaceful way to live our lives from now on. Most people are as good as gold in their minds and hearts, but some are dark and negative, some have hearts as dark as coal. I really like most all people I meet, new and old; however, when one meets a dark-hearted person, it can be a frustrating experience. Especially if that one is in a position of restriction or can deny another in some way something they are in need of. Those people got that way from constant bombardment of questions, pressures, requests and anger from all those they must deal with in the daily systems that were setup to restrict and make demands on otherwise beautiful souls. The hardening of those people in these positions happens over time. You have likely guessed by now that, *yes*, this is due to the use of money, which we already know created greed, force and all the other stuff we have in our daily existence. Those that have to say no to you are being told to do so by the people they work for, this extends all the way to the top of the money chain.

On the flip side there is an analogy of a piece of coal that can pertain to hardened people. If you press a piece of coal hard enough and long enough, you will get a diamond. These hardened people will likely turn out to have the best hearts of gold ever once they release the pressures they place on themselves or have allowed others to place upon them.

I have explained many things in this book. All of which are directly related to the use of money in our society. Putting the use of money under scrutiny, we can see that all the problems of the world are directly related and that the solution is only to get rid of the use of money all together. This will be very hard for most because they are so engrossed and ingrained in the use of it. As I have said before, the end of this use will not come as a result of the mentality of the 20th Century people. However, we are at the beginning of this end.

Whether the people of today realize it or not, we/they will see some upheavals from within the government. This may or may not directly affect you, the readers of this book. But you will be affected indirectly in a conscious way in the trust you may have thought you had in your government and this will shake the very base of your beliefs. When people start to release the trust they have in the system, they will seek out information that points to a better way of living. I too want a better way, but I know it will not be in a system of money. After the release of this money era, we will all start to live in freedom and with stress-free lives.

The government is an outdated dinosaur. Remember, we built it and we can tear it down. However, we cannot do it by fighting with it. It has grown to be too big and strong for any one person or small group to fight. We as humans are already self-governing; we can decide for ourselves what is best for each one of us. No government or any other person can really decide what is best for anyone other than himself or herself as an individual person anyway. The only people that need outside assistance are the handicapped, but they will still be cared for after money is abolished much as they are today. You must know these people have come into life for a particular experience otherwise they would not have come in the way they did.

Fighting the system as it is will only make it stronger because you are giving it your power even more by doing so. The courts and lawyers always find ways to work against the defendant. No matter what the situation is, it is always stacked against the people. If you go to courtrooms and just watch the way things are done, you will see delays and denials of all kinds. This is a waiting game ploy to get you to become discouraged and agree with them or feel intimidated.

Here is a different example of government, if a business is doing well and its making a lot of money it tends to make policies that are not always good for it and its people and sometimes gets an attitude toward the people that support it. It will sometimes throw its weight around and can be unreasonable to the people that support it. Our government treats all people with disdain and an attitude that its constituents are its property. If you fight it directly you will likely get nowhere and in the process you are giving it your power. It matters not what you do to fight this system because they will only come up with some way to defeat you because they are the lawmakers, they prey off the public, and they also do not follow their own laws. They have the brainwashed gun totters they call peacemakers or cops to force you into submission.

When you challenge the law, they will either ignore it or just make a new law that outlaws your challenge. The only way to defeat this monster is to stop feeding it and let it starve to death. If the people that support it stop supporting it, what happens? As with any business, you are now taking all your power back and no longer feeding the monster as you once did. It runs out of money, strength and power, it shrivels up and dies. This is how the government (the *monster*) will be removed from our world. You may say that we need an armed force to defend our shores; I say *no way!* The government causes our need to form an army to protect our selves from other countries. The government creates the wars and anger that our young men die over. If we have no more government, then who is there to make trouble between us and another country? No one. Did any business ever make war with another country? No. Business is out to make money, not war. Only governments make war; they think it is good for business. The people in the armies and public servant jobs will also learn that the orders they are given to control the masses should and will be ignored. If they follow these orders, they will accrue the system's karma and are helping to hold back the evolution of the entire planet and its entire people.

As for the attitudes between countries, when the belief system I have described is a norm for all peoples, there will be no one that will want to conquer or dominate any other country or person. As peace prevails in the hearts of men and women, peace will then prevail all over the earth. It really is funny how government thinks peace is a lack of war.

Government will, as all businesses that are in trouble of extinction do, change the way it treats the people and rewrite and throw away many of its policies and laws, thus becoming more user-friendly. However, we do not need any government to exist on earth. Do you think heaven has a government system? No, they do not have a governmental system at all like we do.

I have explained about free will in chapter four, but I wish to add a bit more in this section for clarity. Free will overrides all the lies and laws that are heaped on people. What do some people think that makes them better than the ones they are trying to persecute? What makes them think it is okay to do whatever they want to another free will person? The answer is nothing, except they have the free will ability to do as one wishes. They will learn this before they can evolve to a higher level. (These words are far truer than you can imagine.) Man has free will and no one can take that away~ever. Even in difficult times, no matter how bad it gets, even when it seems there is no other choice, there still is. A choice will always be available to one, regardless. We may say there is no other choice at times, but this is only because we do not wish to make the choice that would cause harm to us or another in some way. But the choice is always still there.

Freewill: Another perspective
As for freewill we all have it and there is no unseen force that will ever interfere with any choice anyone makes, no matter what that choice is. To demonstrate the existence of free will and non-interference from higher forces, let's use the earlier example of the twin towers destruction and the Columbine school shootings. Now you will all likely agree that the persons forcing there will upon the people they killed created some very heavy karma with each person whose life they ended. Just imagine how many lifetimes they will have to undergo being killed, taken advantage of or whatever is needed to settle the karma with each person that they have harmed. This also includes all the families connected to each person who was killed, due to the grief experienced by the surviving families.

Now, again, did an unseen force come down and stop any of these events because they were wrong? No, it did not. There is no right or wrong in the eyes of God, there is only an imbalance that needs to be brought back into balance. People have been cursing God for eons because they made a judgment that this or that should not have happened to them. They curse God because they think God did not hear or answer their prayers or needs.

147

Man is the one that judges and says you were wrong. The higher forces watching over man just record it all. No judgment is ever made by the higher forces.

God says *do unto others as you would have others do unto you*. This is because we are all created equal and in the likeness of God. This is the rule as given by the higher forces. God did not put us here so the *all that is* could just alter things because we asked for interference from above when we get ourselves into trouble down here. We can however change our own situation at will. It is very easy to do if one is totally sincere in the desire to change, as long as the soul does not override the desired change. An example of that desire would be like the old ways where one would pray to God for a change or maybe a miracle in ones life. If the prayers were sincere enough the change would come about. In reality what one is really doing here is altering ones situation on their own because of the sincerity of the desire to make the change. Sincerity is felt not thought. The feeling center automatically gets this when it is real the higher realms then see this sincerity and energies start to move around the situation to create a positive change in accordance with the desire. This might seem like God has granted you a miracle.

Karma plays out for those that are in need of balance at some future time as it may be needed. This too can be a good reason that the *all that is* or ones sincerity has not altered one's situation. The higher forces do not judge us in any way or interfere because we have been created with free will to choose, as we will. If one chooses to harm or force their will upon another, which is against the higher rules that be, they will have to settle that choice at some future time. As others join into a situation, they also take on a portion of, add to, and perpetuate the karma.

Freewill cancels out choices made by another involving the one. In other words, when a person makes a choice that involves another person but that other person makes a choice not to do what the first person wants, the first choice is canceled out because it is against the will of the second person. No one can make a choice for another person against his or her will; if they do, it is a forced situation. If a choice is made for another, but both agree upon it, then no harm is done. In the former a higher directive comes into play when the imbalance and karma is created that must be later settled between the two people. An outside force such as a court cannot ever settle the karma unless it is asked for and agreed upon by the two parties settling the karma. If this does not happen, it will only create a heavier payback and draw the people involved in the court or legal system into the karma. This only makes matters worse. If you think about this it just makes common sense.

[Ms. Alison addresses the class.]

Ms. Alison:
Okay, class, that was a long chapter. Our time for today is almost up, so we will continue with this tomorrow as a review. Maybe you will want to re-read this tonight.

[The next day.]

Ms. Alison:
Good morning, class. I am going to throw out the question to the class, what did you learn from this chapter? Anyone?

Jimmy:
I will go first, Ms. Alison.

Ms. Alison:
Okay, Jimmy.

Jimmy:
We can see that an important shift of their time was a major change in consciousness and evolution, but it seems as if most people did not know much if anything about what was going on behind the scenes, especially the system. The system may have known, but it appears it wasn't going to act on it to make any positive change for the people. He has said in prior chapters that he thought they did know but were too stupid and arrogant to recognize it. They probably thought they could maintain what they had no matter what the people did. The fact that no past civilization has lasted for a very long time is important to note, because they seemed to mess up with the people all the time and the people have torn down every one so far, as they also did this one. It would appear that the people are always the supreme decision makers no matter what system they build or how that system may turn on the people. When he talked about the exponential learning, I thought about the falling rock where they are at or near maximum velocity for their evolution period.

I have read about the prior civilizations that predate any of the earlier known people the author wrote about for his time period. We have proof of societies that go back about two million years before our time. They were also very advanced in technology and it appears they blew themselves up somehow. I guess the whole process must have started all over again from scratch. I wonder who or what restarted life again? In comparison I think we have finally made it past the blowing ourselves up routine I hope. We do not currently have the destructive weapons like they had. Our defensive means for any outside interference that I am aware of are from other off-world civilizations that may come to earth to move in on us to take our planet. I do not believe it is likely that this situation would ever happen. I do know that our defenses do not consist of nuclear power like back in the money era. Even though we haven't heard of any aliens yet, that doesn't mean they aren't out there.

Ms. Alison:
Jimmy, that is fairly correct, but I wish to add that one or more of those very old civilizations did not blow themselves up as most did. The Lumarians did not do that instead they evolved so highly that they left the physical reality of existence. Many were killed when Atlantis supposedly sunk. The rest just moved to another dimension that we can't see with our physical eyes. As for how civilizations regenerated in the past, there were sometimes pockets of humans who survived these annihilations; it was those surviving pockets who started the next civilizations. At some of the far earlier times there were reseedings by outside forces.

Jimmy, I want to spread this around the class so let's have someone else take the next section. Who is going next?

Alice:
I will take the next section, Ms. Alison.

Ms. Alison:
Okay, Alice.

Alice:
The author talks about karma and evolution being intermixed. I agree with the way he put it, but it is still only a small part of evolution. However, he did say that bad karma could hold one from evolving at all until it is rebalanced. I can see how this would affect the person in question. He then talks about

time compression and that we are all a physical part of the planet itself. Today time is even shorter because we have another one and a half to two hours less time in our days than the author had in his day. Since this book was written, scientists have been able to measure time compression so we know this to be a fact today. This has nothing to do with the amount of sunlight in a day it has more to do with the cosmic clock of the universe. We have been able to measure our relationship to the energy of the planet giving us a *signature*, so to speak, of our source of creation, proving that our bodies did come from and exist only by means of the mother Gaia in ways we can measure beyond just the obvious facts where we come from the chemicals of earth. Then he talks about karma being a test. I agree and can reaffirm that this is still the way it works today. I have done things to my little brother and have found that I get paid back almost right away. It may be that something will happen a few days later that makes me think of what I did to my brother, but I always regret messing things up for myself by acting foolishly or in a negative way toward other people. So I see that instant karma does come back to us—I think even faster now than it did when this book was written, which is probably directly related to time compression. I think everyone in this room will agree that karma comes back on them swiftly.

[Class mumbles and chuckles in agreement.]

It proves that the free will test he spoke of exists and karma is the balancing tool for it.

One thing I can say with confidence is that I really don't like that legal system he speaks so much about. We can also see that we do not have the authority to interfere in another person's choices or to harm and or manipulate them. Our way today is of non-interference and of letting people be who they are. I have looked up the old legal meaning of the word "person" and compared it to our dictionary, today it does not say that people are corporations, instead it says we are humans.

Ms. Alison:
Great, Alice
Who is going next?

Allan:
I will, Ms. Alison.

Ms. Alison:
Good, Allan.

Allan:
First I would like to see a camel pass through the eye of a needle.

[Class chuckles.]

Allan:
Okay. Seriously, the church thing was just as bad or maybe even a little worse in some areas than the legal system was. It seems to me that the churches may have started out okay, but over time they became manipulative and then they wanted to control the people. From reading the rest of this book, and some other history articles, I see they gained competition from the governmental systems. They even warred over this at times. It seems from what I've read that the systems had won these wars for the most part because the churches were under control of the money and laws and since they had to use money, they were just as controlled by the laws as the masses. He also states that the system or government wanted to kill God so the government could become God in its place. We have none of that stuff today. We just live and let live as we are directed by our understanding of free will and non-interference.

Ms. Alison:
Thank you, Allan. Well who is up for the next part?

Ron:
Me.

Ms. Alison:
Okay, Ron.

Ron:
This is a short part, but it says a fair amount about evolution. If those people back then kept doing what they had been doing for so long, they would have blown themselves up and we would not be here today talking about evolution. Maybe we would be living in caves starting all over again.

[Class laughter.]

So we can see that change is important and inevitable. I think we will last quite a long time now that we are past the warring stages of existence.

Ms. Alison:
Very good, Ron. Who will be next?

Gerald:
I guess I should join this conversation, Ms. Alison.

Ms. Alison:
I was wondering if you were going to speak up, Gerald.

Gerald:
I was not going to, but this has become interesting and I can't help agreeing about so many of the coincidences that were written about before it all happened–by that I mean all that came about a great deal of time later. Especially since the future can't be predicted with any accuracy. In regards to the section on peace I cannot understand that phrase that says we are free because our troops fought for it. That doesn't make sense because they were fighting each other from country to country and sometimes among people within the same country, like the civil war. How did they figure they were free if they kept starting wars with each other over and over again? True peace is a state of being within a person, not a lack of something external.

Ms. Alison:
Gerald, they fought among each other because they could not agree with each other about money and control. Governments tried to control people and the people would not stand for it.

Gerald:
Oh, I see Ms. Alison.

Ms. Alison:
Please go on, Gerald.

Gerald:
Thank God we are all in agreement on this today. I cannot comment on the big mistake the government was supposed to make back then, because I do not know what it was. I have never heard or read any one particular thing that caused the people to turn away from the system that tore it down. Whatever it

was, I am glad we did get through it. Maybe it was just a one-more-straw-on-the-camel's-back thing that caused the people to turn away. However, we are proof that the people prevailed again for the more peaceful time that we live in today. I like his analogy of the coal and diamond, but I would not want to be that coal under all that pressure from others. I guess the last thing I remember is the part that describes how they built the government and they could tear it down. They sure did, didn't they? I agree that the people are always going to be the supreme decision makers since we are the creators of whatever system is in existence at any given time.

Ms. Alison:
Thank you, Gerald. Well, we have one more section of this chapter. Who is next?

Fran:
I will take this, Ms. Alison.

Ms. Alison:
Okay, Fran.

Fran:
I understood from reading this section that the government back then was a real monster and out of control. I guess they created it and fed it and then it bit through its leash, and attacked the people and started eating them. It then left its droppings all over everything and everyone all over the country. When it got restless, it moved on to other countries to eat and drop on them too. Personally, I like talking about the lighter side of things, such as the second perspective he gives on free will. In this he talks about the unseen force that did not come and stop anything from ever happening. We know today that our world and universe is one that allows us to grow and do as we please on a very abundant planet. It's a good thing we are not on Jupiter where there are few life sustaining properties. The plan of evolution, I think, is a good one. I understand that free will does cancel out anyone else's will because the person has total control over his own life. We are all the same in those respects, so how can someone's free will override another's if we all have the same ability to choose?

Like Alice, I can tell when I accrue karma that I later have to balance, because

I get a similar feeling like he described in an earlier chapter about balancing karma. Well that's about it, Ms. Alison.

Ms. Alison:
Well, class, that wraps up the day. Since the school year started off in the middle of the week we have a short first week, so I will see you all Monday I trust.

Sharon:
Ms. Alison, Alice and I are going to do a past life regression tomorrow.

Ms. Alison:
That's right, Sharon. You will have to tell us about it on Monday.

Sharon:
Okay. We will.

[Monday morning.]

Ms. Alison:
Good morning, class. How was everybody's weekend? Good, I hope. Sharon, we are all waiting to hear what happened in the regression session you and Alice had. First, I want to say that our book is taking a turn for the future and the higher realms of consciousness. After we hear from Alice and Sharon, we will go on to the next chapter.

Sharon, please get comfortable and tell us how it went.

Sharon:
First I couldn't go with Alice, but Sandra called to see if she could join us, so the two of us went instead. Sandra got to go first.

Ms. Alison:
Sandra, would you please tell us your story first since you were the first one in.

Sandra:
Okay. We went into a small, quiet room with a comfortable chair where Christine, the instructor, had me get comfortable. We began and she took me into a relaxed state. I remember I was feeling pretty good and relaxed. Then she asked me to go back several lifetimes. I guess I went back about fifty

155

lifetimes. She asked me to look around the room to see where I was. At first it was dark and cold, but then it got a little lighter so I could see enough to know where I was. It was nasty~I was in a jail with bars and smelly air. It was very filthy and I got upset with what I was seeing. I was also a man with a beard and ragged clothes. Christine noticed I was disturbed and she asked me to move out of that lifetime and go back further.

She said to go as far back as I wanted until I got to a place I liked. So I traveled way back to a time where I saw a reflection of a woman in a pool of water. The image was beautiful. I suddenly realized it was me and I was a tall, strong athletic woman with long blond hair; I wore leather and skins and carried a huge sword that I probably couldn't lift today. Christine asked me to look around at my surroundings to see where I was. When I did, I saw several other women and a few men who seemed to be waiting for me. There was a pentagram marked on the ground with stones and a fire burning next to that. There was a hut with a grass roof, but no glass in the windows, just holes. I started speaking Gaelic to the group as I taught them about magic. It turns out that I was a coven leader of a magic group. My name was Shalandra. Everyone looked up to me with great respect and amazement. I gathered that I was a great warrior princess and a high priestess of magic. It was really cool. That remembrance made me forget about the jail I was in before that. My session lasted about 20 minutes then it was Sharon's turn. The instructor brought me out slowly and asked me how it felt and if this was my first time regressing, because I seemed to do it so easily. That was about all I can remember right now.

Ms. Alison:
Sharon, what did you get from this experience?

Sharon:
I was upset at the fact that I lived in a jail under such horrible conditions. The other life was way better even though they were fighters because they all carried swords and knives~I guess for protection from others trying to take their possessions. I was comfortable in that role, but today I would not want to fight with them or anybody else. I think we have moved past that way of thinking, because it seems barbaric to us today.

Ms. Alison:
Well, Alice, what was your experience?

Alice:
I went through all the same stuff to get into a relaxed state. Then the instructor asked me to choose a time I wanted to go to before we got down to the regression. I chose to go to the same era that our class book was written. I wanted to see if I was alive then. She told me to drift back to the year 2004. When I looked around, I was in a house and in a bed that seemed comfortable. Then I was in the hallway listening to another girl in the bathroom brushing her teeth. Suddenly I heard a loud crash downstairs, followed by loud shouting over something I couldn't make out. At this point the girl came out of the bathroom and walked by me saying, "There they go again." I didn't quite understand, so I followed the girl into another room and asked her what she meant by that. She replied, "What are you, lame today? It's Mom and Dad fighting again about how much it costs to repair the car, I think. Anyway, they will be mad for days so we should steer clear of them as much as possible, Sis."

I remember thinking that I have never heard my parents do that. I was still curious about being there, so I went downstairs to look around, but there was no one there. I went outside and saw some antique cars going by that mostly looked brand-new. That was cool. But then a boy came up to me and said, "Bess, we need to get going–if we wait we'll be late for school again. If I'm late one more time, the school is going to turn me into the juvenile office and my parents will get fined this time, so let's go. If my dad has to pay another fine, he will whip my ass again." The boy was cute, but I guess I drifted away from that time as I heard the instructor asking me where I was now. She then asked me to come back to the present and our session was over. It's a little fuzzy now, but I think there was more detail in the surroundings when I was there than I can remember.

Ms. Alison:
Sharon, tell us what you got from your experience?

Sharon:
At first, I was a little out of it from the noises I heard, then it got heavier when that boy showed up because he was angry and pushy toward me. I didn't like that at all. He seemed to be in trouble all the time, I guess. I felt out of place feeling the sensations that were being forced at me. I never got to see my mom, so that was a little disappointing. I wanted to see what she was like. I guess that is about all I can say about that experience. Except that it was really

not very pleasant having an intense situation thrown at me like that.

Ms. Alison:
Okay, class, that was interesting. We should move onto the next chapter now.

Philip:
Hello, Ms. Alison.

[A boy enters the classroom.]

Ms. Alison:
Hello, your name is?

Philip:
I am late I know, but it was unavoidable, because I was in Australia backpacking this summer. Oh, my name is Phillip.

Ms. Alison:
Well, Phillip, please take a seat. Do you know what we are studying?

Philip:
Yes. I have been monitoring the class on my communications unit, so I am pretty much up to speed.

Ms. Alison:
May I ask why you are so late since school started last week?

Philip:
Well, in line with the class lesson, I need to say that with all the people traveling all over the world today, it is a little hard to get accommodations on short notice. Especially if you forget to make travel plans well ahead of when you need them. I just forgot. I checked for a travel seat a week and a half ago, but that was just too late to get here on time. I was supposed to check three weeks ago to get a seat for the right time I needed but with all the fun I was having I just forgot.

Ms. Alison:
Since we are doing a comparison of the money era and now, can you tell us about traveling now compared to traveling in the past when money was used?

Philip:
Yes, Ms. Alison.
As I recall from what I caught on my communication unit and what I have read prior, travel back then occurred less frequently than today. Traveling was prohibitive because so much money was needed to pay for tickets and accommodations—and then there were the restrictions of entering another country where you needed permission in writing or something like that. It was all rather restrictive. I have heard that you could not even go to some countries because they were warring with each other. Today that is all a thing of the past. All we need to do is ask out communications unit to tell us what accommodations are available for the place we want to go; it tells us and we plan for the times that are available. We then go to the airport and find the gate for the plane and get on. When we get to the other destination, we get a car or have a cab drive us if we do not want to go find a car. I like the cabs because the drivers usually know all the good food places and the sights and will suggest a lot of stuff if you ask. You can always get a car at the hotel later if you want.

Ms. Alison:
Phillip, what about the passports they needed in the money era?

Philip:
What do you mean, Ms. Alison? We all live on this planet together. Oh, that's the permission paper I mentioned earlier, isn't it? Why would I need something like a passport to go anywhere in the world of people since we are all the same?

Ms. Alison:
Class, I wish to explain that back in the era of money, people had to go through the process of getting a passport that gave them permission to travel. These documents had your picture and originating country listed on them and every country you went to had to stamp your passport to prove you were there and also allow you to enter that country. When they checked to see if your papers were in order, they could reject your entry into their country if they wanted to. They called this *going through customs* to get into and out of a country. This was a great burden to most travelers and took a lot of time to deal with. Personally, I think it was a waste of energy.

Okay, class, I think it is time to go to the next chapter. Phillip, since you are so late getting here, you have been elected to read this to the class.

Philip:
Okay, Ms. Alison.

Chapter Nine

[Phillip reads to the class.]
How things really work on earth and in the higher realms

I don't like using many of the phrases and sayings from the religious texts because they are so misinterpreted, and there is little assurance that any of it is real for us today as compared to the days when these phrases were taught. Many of the messages of that time, as have been previously stated in another chapter, are out-dated for today's people and our level of evolutionary understandings. This is like comparing technology of the 1950s to the technology of 2005, or the beliefs of people that thought the world was flat to the beliefs and views of the world from a space station today.

Things in the higher realms do not work as they say in the churches. Yes, it is true that things can be created that originate from a thought. And, yes, people can move objects with their minds by directing energy. But things that are taught in the churches (such as the return of Christ) are completely wrong, because they misinterpreted it, either on purpose or by mistake. If on purpose, it was to control the masses so they would think that they needed the church in order to get to heaven. The real meaning of the returning of Christ is quite different. It is in the phrase that says, "You will do greater things than I." This was spoken by Christ himself and it means that when the Christ returns (or when that energy reawakens, as it is more clearly articulated), it will be inside of each and every person alive on earth. Jesus is not coming back as a single man—rather, the energy of the Christ consciousness is coming to all people that are alive at the time it happens. In fact, it is already here for everybody but only some of us have tapped into this stream.

How far is heaven? There is a popular song that came out around 2003 with this tile. The answer is *not far, not far at all*. You see heaven is right inside of you, right where it has been all the time. It's just waiting for us to turn to it and embrace it and it will embrace us right back.

Science Revisited

I spoke earlier in the book of a light in all things at a very small micron level that science has recently discovered. What is this light? It is the very essence of the *all that is*. The very fabric of what makes up everything we know in this universe. Both science and medical science will discover a very important relation to how all things work and how creation is possible from this light. In a sense, you could say science has found God. Or maybe the headlines will read, *Science Finds the Light.*

This light is the energy of all things; it is what creates and maintains all things. It is an intelligent source of energy. This intelligence resides in the paper of this book in your hand and in your hand that is holding this book. It is in your eyes that read these words and all other things. *Yes,* that means God resides within *you.* Remember, "Lift a stone and you will find me, split a piece of wood and I am there." The energy of God is in everything.

Another phenomenon is the shifting of the true North Pole. Science is a bit bewildered by this. That shifting has caused some unusual things to happen in recent times. These events have come to completion, so we will not likely see them again. These phenomena were caused by the shifting of the magnetic grids of the earth by an unseen force that came to earth just for that purpose. The grids were moved east/west a bit to realign earth to the star called the Great Central Sun, which cannot be seen from earth's location and perspective at this time. The shift was also to rebalance the earth herself. The result of this shifting caused many animals to go off course, so to speak. It resulted in the beaching of the whales and porpoise for several years. These animals were not lost. Animals follow by instinct an invisible set of magnetic lines that crisscross the planet as a grid. These are called *lay lines.* The reason they ran ashore is that the lay lines they instinctively follow were moved when the grid was shifted, which caused the lines to go across land instead of out in the ocean where they were previously located. The whales and porpoises had to realign to the new grids by following new lines that kept them out in the deeper waters. As we know, some whales that were pushed off the beaches came right back because they were following the same lay line and re-beached themselves again. After a short time they did learn to realign to the deeper water grids.

This shifting is also in line with the consciousness of people. It has had some effects, but not anything that can be measured by our current science that is directly related to this shift. But a shift nonetheless has occurred in the way humans think and perceive all that is around them. This shift took place from 1989 to early 2002. This shift has brought new information into our world that previously could not have entered. The specific details of that information are not for the scope of this book. However that information has resulted in the ability and need for writing this book.

Indigo children

The children of the future are already coming in at this time. In fact, the world is being flooded with them now. They are called the *Indigo Children* (though not all children being born are Indigos). The next wave, which has already started is the wave of the *Crystal Children*. These children will be the real movers and shakers of earth. These people have a very different outlook on life. Both the Indigos and the *Crystal Children* carry the genetics for future changes. When the time comes for them to move into rolls of leadership, many changes will occur all over the earth. Our job is to encourage them and nourish their understandings. There is a book written by Lee Carol called *The Indigo Children* that describes the needs of these young people.

Changing times

We must break down the barriers of the old ways. We must move out of that era and into a new age of living to embrace life instead of remaining a slave of the old system of control. This new way will solidify in our consciousness as we turn away from the old ways. You may be wondering why the *all that is* doesn't just make things better for us? There is a reason for the way things are, but that reason is not for the scope of this book. What this book does cover is the re-awareness of the mind and soul to rejoin and reawaken as one. It is time for human awareness on earth to evolve out of its stagnation. Both the light workers of today and the new people spoken of earlier are the shape shifters of this earth reality. They will reclaim their power from an old system and make way for an even higher level of consciousness to come after them. There are always endings and beginnings to all things in life. Please catch the wave of the future now and let's get on with the transformation of *this* reality into the *new* reality of a gentler way of living on earth.

The movie *The Matrix* is an entertaining movie to watch and is not by any means true in the sense it is portrayed, but the control portrayed in the movie is very real in regards to people today. This movie shows a person breaking through the barriers, which is a must for us to evolve. Sometimes we need a little help like the help Neo got form Morpheus to get out of the illusion he was living; however, he was not *living* but merely generating energy for something else (the machines) that was controlling him.

If you watch this movie in the right perspective, it will be a very spiritual movie. It may even spark or trigger some things within you that you never saw or realized before.

Biology bubbles

We humans walk around on earth thinking we are separate from all other people. However, this is far from the actual truth of the matter. You are as much a part of the person next to you as that person's hair or hand is a part of them. We walk around in physical, biological units called bodies thinking we are separate from one another but we are not. To the naked eye it appears that way. Remember, the science section earlier where science has found light at a molecular level. That energy is also in every molecule of air too. It's like a blanket of fog that permeates the entire universe. Remember, it is what created and binds all things together. That energy is a constant everywhere. It's just that we have the ability to walk around through the air and over the earth that makes us think we are separate from one another. Human biology vibrates at a certain rate but other living things, such as trees, vibrate at a different rate or frequency. This causes the sense of separation. When you eat foods, what are you really eating? Science says your body is taking in vitamins and minerals, but what else is in this food? Yes, the energy of all creation is in this food. It is also in the air we breathe. You are taking this energy in along with all the other vibrations in the vitamins and minerals. The body burns energy and so it needs to replenish that energy through food. In time we will no longer need food; we will get our energy straight from the air we breathe. So in reality we are all the same, the same energy from the same source of that light energy. What you do to another, you are also actually doing to yourself.

By doing something negative to another against his will creates an imbalance in the energy flow. Remember the section on karma; this imbalance must go back into balance before things can move forward. This energy has created the universe, the human body and your consciousness, plus the free will within that consciousness. We only seem to be cut off from that energy, but it was by design that this seems to be that way. As you now know, in reality we are not at all separate. It was all for our personal human experience that we appear to be separate from one another. This separation experience has allowed us to evolve far faster than we could have if we did not have this experience. The in-depth reasons for the separations are beyond this book. However, you can access that energy at any time you wish. Some people do it through meditation, others do it just by relaxing, and others read inspiring words written by other people that are in touch with that energy at core levels within themselves.

Accessing this energy is as simple as consciously breathing and paying attention to the in and out movement of the breath while also paying attention to what is behind the breath and any energetic presence that is felt while breathing. This presence will seem to have substance. This will quiet the mind and still the nerves and put one at peace. Doing this can have the effect of washing away all one's cares and worries almost instantly. When you make contact you will completely cleanse yourself of a great deal of stress. This only takes a few minutes to do. The part people find hard about this is wondering too much whether or not they are doing it right or letting their minds wander onto other things. One needs only to let go of that and concentrate on the breath and what is behind it on an energy level.

Ms. Alison:
Thank you, Phillip. Class, what did we get from this in relation to what we have and know in our reality?
Ron:
Ms. Alison? I would like to say a few words about this chapter.

Ms. Alison:
Yes, Ron.

Ron:
The part in the beginning about the religious phrases I found interesting. I think we have let all of that old stuff go, especially since it doesn't feel right to us today. He apparently had done that or he could not have written this book. He couldn't have understood these things and written this book if he still believed in the religious texts of the past. I know we do not have these teachings anymore in our day.

I understand the part of relating technology and past religious teachings to today. I agree that they really needed to drop the old ways of thinking long before they actually did because they did not fit with the evolution that was required for us to get where we are now. I think that has held us back too, we would be farther along the path of evolution if they did no hold onto the old was for so long. I cannot relate to their consciousness levels back then, but it seems they operated with a heavier and a more rigid type of mentality.

Sandra:
Ms. Alison, I would like to say something about that.

Ms. Alison:
Yes, Sandra.

Sandra:
I want to comment on the part Ron was talking about where he said the mentality must have been heavy and rigid. When I did that regression and I went to that jail, I remember feeling a very heavy, controlled feelings and rigid thinking in the person I was back then. It was very difficult for me to relate to that from my understanding of life because we do not have that kind of control in our lives. I think that I was in that prison for some really insignificant reason, but it seemed that he/I was not getting out too soon. That feeling of being helpless and under the control of something that hated or did not have any compassion for human life was really unbearable. I can see an old way in this experience that must have been very hard at times on the people of that time.

Ms. Alison:
Thank you, Sandra. Is there anyone else that would like to pick up from here?

Peter:
Yes. I would.

Ms. Alison:
Okay, Peter.

Peter:
Well, I have skipped to the end of this book and read the author's comments and would like to comment on the *How Far is Heaven* section. I won't tell you the last part of the book, but I agree with the author about the fact that heaven really is right inside of us all the time. I have experienced it in my life when I go to that place he speaks about later in the book. I don't know how many people back then did this or how successful they were, but it feels like soaring through the universe sometimes and other times it is like becoming very intertwined with the energies of the *all that is*. I lose myself sometimes in the feelings. When that happens, I seem to lose all track of time and even my body feels like it is part of the universe.

Ms. Alison:
Thanks, Peter. Anyone else care to speak up on the next part of this chapter?

Sally:
I will take the next part, Ms. Alison.

Ms. Alison:
Okay, Sally.

Sally:
What Peter said is directly related to the part in science where this book explains the energy source. Then it goes on to talk about the whales beaching themselves. I have read about that happening back then. It seems that the people then did not understand what was really happening. They still believed, it would seem, that the world was flat compared to what we understand of the entire process of life and energy today. I think there were very few people like the author that understood or knew about any of the higher workings of life back then. From my understanding most people were what they called asleep.

As for the Indigos, my great grandparents were Indigos from what my mother says. She said they had a better life than their earlier family did, but still not what we have now. She said they made some interesting discoveries in their time. They were some of the barrier breakers of there time. I guess they taught thousands about a higher understanding and helped them move out of the money era to some degree. I have seen that old movie the author talks about, *The Matrix*, and I thought it was interesting that a movie like that was even made back then.

Ms. Alison:
Sally, that was interesting, wasn't it. But the people of that time did not realize the correlation of the messages in that movie to their evolution for the most part. They just watched it because it was entertaining. As for the few people back then that were more like the author was, I must say that there was far more of them than we might think from reading just this book. The author was just one of thousands but still that was a small percentage of the population as a whole.

Please, you have the floor Sally. Continue.

Sally:
I have to agree with the next part about the biology bubbles. I have also felt the things Peter described, but a little differently for me, as it is different for each person. I feel separate from all of you here but I know I am not at all separate. But it is fun to think we are or at least know we have the ability to think we are separate. But I would not want to be totally separate like they thought they were back in the money era. That must have been a lonely feeling thinking you were all by yourself. From reading this book I can see that this is the way it must have been. I can see how some might have gone a little, or maybe a lot, mad at times feeling disconnected from the energy of the *all that is*. I know I can feel that connection right now while I am speaking to you. I know that if I mess with someone in a negative way against their will, I am drawing the same negativity toward myself and that I will have to balance that in some way before I can get past what I did. Not to mention how I would be holding back myself as well as the other person. I see this as if I were tugging on a blanket--the same blanket everyone is under--when I pull hard on it, it takes some away from others both near to me and on the far side of the blanket. My pulling is like karma: where the blanket needs to be pulled back the other way to balance it again, I must let my grip on it ease up so it can be pulled back into place, or rebalanced again. Today we understand that when we hold another back in some way, we are holding ourselves back at the same time.

The energy I am feeling right now is coming from my connection to my breath in a way we all learned when we were young so we would not go into the feelings of isolation that were so prevalent in the past eras. It is so much a part of me that I do not even think about it, it is just there all the time.

Ms. Alison:
Thank you, Sally. Class, that wraps up this chapter. Let's do the last chapter tomorrow. Please read Chapter Ten, *The Power of True Belief* tonight.

[The following day.]

Ms. Alison:
Good morning, class. Has everyone read this chapter? Great. I want to re-read

this chapter to the class because it talks about what is possible in life. I feel that this holds true for us as much as it did for the money era people. We too are still evolving and we always will be as long as we are in the physical.
[Ms. Alison reads to the class.]

Chapter Ten

The power of true belief

I would like to take things to another level for the final chapter of this book. What is impossible? The answer is nothing. What you believe are the only limitations you have. The mind can create anything you wish in your life, be it more money or better health or a change in your surroundings or whatever you wish. It's all a matter of your deepest core beliefs that you hold as the basis for your current existence. These core beliefs create your reality, or, I should say, your world as you live in it.

What do you believe? What has been taught to you is what you know. Is there anything beyond what you were taught? The answer is *yes*. But will you let your mind believe beyond the box you currently live in? It is difficult for many people to let go of the beliefs they have lived with for so long. I, the author, am one that did believe in the limitations of the mind as it was taught during my upbringing, but have since stepped out of that box and into a very different perception of reality. My new reality is very different and uplifting from the old one.

A good example of this is well-defined in the movie *The Matrix*. The mind makes things real for one if one believes what the mind is saying. For example, Neo could not make the jump from one building to another because his mind kept telling him that it was impossible. Yet Morpheus made the jump with ease. This demonstrates two very different beliefs: one believes it is possible and the other believes it is not, so one fails under this belief, while the other one succeeds.

We live in a time of many unseen changes in humanity and the world. We are in the beginning of a change that will bring the earth into a new level of evolution. This level has not happened before because we have for the most part destroyed ourselves in past civilizations prior to the current known history of earth and man. We have passed the point of self-destruction this time. This is what is so interesting for us now. Our job now is to evolve into a new era of peace and change that takes us away from the old ways.

In this new era there will be a difference between thinking things and knowing things. One example of this is Neo in the movie *The Matrix* and another is seen in the studies done on rich people who came from poverty. A similar answer was given to the question, "How did you make it?" The answer was "I always knew I would get here." What they are saying is that there was a core belief within them that they would get to the rich man's side of the fence. They held this as a truth deep within themselves and life never swayed this truth for them. For many people life does change the beliefs one holds through bombardment with negative events and money difficulties that comes from the mass consciousness. But for those who became rich, that never happened. Since these people were not swayed in their beliefs, they made the subtle alterations in their life that brought the riches into their life. Neo always had it in him to believe, but he was unsure of himself for a while; when he changed that belief, he began doing things he previously believed to be impossible.

What one currently believes at the deepest levels of the mind is what one is currently experiencing in one's life. When you truly believe in something you go about your life making subtle moves, changes and adjustments on a subconscious level that moves you in ways that create your beliefs and manifest reality for you. The lyrics of a popular song of the 20th Century has a phrase that goes, "If you want to change your life then change your mind." This is very true for all people. However, this may be harder to do than the phrase may suggest. It starts in the mind, usually from a problem that exists in ones external life. There are other internal issues that stem from past lives and from programming of the mind during childhood of the current life. Many times because we have had those beliefs for so long and they are now so ingrained in us over so much time and reinforced in us by training from the outside world, we have a hard time releasing them or changing our patterns and ways of doing things in the world, even though we want to do just that. Others react to your beliefs that you project out into the world. What you send out and what you get back from other people continues to reinforce your reality. It is all based on you and your beliefs from the beginning.

Money! what good is it?

When you have money it gives a feeling of superiority over others. When you don't have money it gives a feeling of inferiority. So what good is it if it creates an unequal set of emotions that constantly throws people out of balance from one extreme to the other? When people are without money for a long time, especially when they need more of it, they tend to entertain dark thoughts. When people that have a lot of money in the money thinking era are comfortable with that money, they tend to belittle others that don't have very much money. <u>So what good is it?</u> Our mental states are such that we need to raise our vibratory levels of understanding up and beyond that way of treating others.

Those that have money and good luck in life will likely not read a book like this, but those that struggle over money will very likely read a book like this. Most people in the world today are struggling over money in some ways, possibly many ways. A wealthy person may find this book in their hands for other reasons in their life that they are seeking answers to.

Nobody helps anybody on this planet when it comes to money. It's all about money! When someone gives money to someone else or to a foundation they do it for the tax benefits they get from the donation. Again, this is about money. When the foundation gives money, it is also for the tax benefits. Again, this is about money. When banks loan money, they do it for the money they will get back from the customer. Again, this is about money. When the government gives money they do it for two reasons: one is for the money they will get back and the other is for the control they will gain. Again, this is about money. The latter is when they give money to other countries. They are purchasing control in that country. When family members help family, they do it for what they expect to get back, either in money or some other area like respect or recognition of sorts. Nobody helps anybody on this planet. It's all about money and control.

Even when money is no more, it will still be about what one expects to get back by helping another. Be it a service performed or something similar. It will still be about what one is expecting to get back in return for what was given. Money just won't be involved anymore and this will make all the difference. Our evolution will come to a time where we as humans will give without expecting a return, this will not come soon, but it will come. The removal of money will have great benefits for all in freedom and release of excess control and oppression from other people that feel they are superior because they have money or control. This money makes them think they have power over others.

Your beliefs hold true in all areas of your life and society as a whole. If you believe we need wars, money, governments, crime, rich people, poor people, etc., you are then reinforcing the whole system that is a manifestation of the beliefs of the mass consciousness of a nation and of the world. The mass consciousness is what keeps the world as it is now. When we as a group change our minds, the whole world will change for the better or the worse,

175

depending on the direction of shift. It is not necessary for the entire world to make a change, but at least 30 percent or more would be required to make an effective change in the entire consciousness of the world reality. This happens one soul and one mind at a time.

This book was written from a higher perspective with many years of personal experiences dealing with money, people, and what happens between people by using money. There is much more to come in future generations that the scope of this book does not cover, but it does indicate some of what we can expect and what our children can expect to come both in our lives and future ones. What we dwell upon is what we create.

The media has a great deal to do with what we dwell upon. Who is controlling what is in the media? The invisible ones behind the scenes are pulling all the strings in an effort to continue controlling us as they have been for many centuries. Why do you think there are regulatory systems? They exist so the string pullers can control what is in the media and all other things as well. The government controls what is reported and, as you probably know, if any station goes beyond that they are put out of business instantly. Do you think a station really needs a license to put a person in front of a camera or microphone and talk to the public telling them what is happening around them? No, they do not. That license does not make a person better qualified to talk. But it does limit what one can say, or they will face persecution from the regulatory agency or even jail in some cases just for telling it like it really is.

The ones behind these agencies are the ones with all the money and power: the bankers, the governments, the law enforcement, and secret agencies etc. are the ones that create and finance wars, most of this money comes from the families that own the world banks. There are approximately six families around the world who own these banks, the banking cartel as it is called. These people and their agencies will not be able to maintain their secret existence to hide what they are really doing for much longer. We need not be concerned with who they are as they will reveal themselves one at a time as deemed appropriate by higher forces in the coming times. The new energies of awareness are revealing some of them already. They will be finding themselves in the news and facing public scrutiny regardless of the regulatory systems. News travels very fast by mouth and by Internet these days. They will soon have a very difficult time coping in the world with the new awareness of people. They will not want to let go of their old ways that have worked for so long for them. What will you choose in your future? To be like the controlling ones or to be a person who lives in harmony on earth with those who are our family of humans? There is a distinction between the controllers and non-controllers. It is not likely that a person of the controller side will choose to even read this material, let alone observe the changes that are taking place now or the new energies now becoming so prevalent on earth. These changes and energies will make their ways (what we are experiencing now) extinct.

True power of belief continued

It's an amazing power. God created the universe because He not only believed He could, but because He knew He could. Just believing in something doesn't always make it happen. It won't happen until you believe it so much that you know it, or know it will manifest like the rich man question above. They got rich because they had true belief, which is *knowing* it will manifest no matter what they do in life. Another view is that a person can believe in his choice to become a doctor. At first this is only a choice one has made, which may be followed by applying oneself to the study of medicine. This person puts in many hours of hard work and study for several years and maybe they even get good grades in medical school. One may find it difficult at times to cope with the study and work that it takes to get through medical school. Maybe one even takes a break from school due to the difficulties one may be having, or maybe one fails some classes. In spite of these difficulties, this person still believes in becoming a doctor.

This situation can arise when a person believes in himself or herself, but the belief is not 100% in ones mind and heart. On the flip side is the student that has 100% belief or true belief in oneself to the point that one just knows one will become a doctor. One goes through school with ease, and remembers and understands everything quickly and with little difficulty.

The person that already has 100% true belief, or what is called *knowing*, doesn't have to wonder one just knew that it would happen. The other person struggles because there is doubt of some kind that comes from a fear or core issue that is holding one back somehow.

Recognition of the issue at the core level has the effect of releasing the issue. This discovery and recognition automatically releases the issue. This must be done without fear because fear will destroy the release, causing one to revert back into the old belief, which may even make it harder to release at a later time.

The only difference between the two students is the amount of belief. One has total belief and the other does not. The other doubts oneself. Everyone has likely experienced this knowing in some area and time in one's life. You need to draw on those experiences and try to discover how it was you believed at that time and recreate that for the now so you can make changes in your beliefs at will. Fear destroys everything before it gets a chance to ever get started. Fear is the biggest roadblock one can have. It might just be a fear of change or maybe a fear of success? When you do make the change in your beliefs 100%, you actually start creating and a stirring the energies of creation to manifest what you want. This then starts a chain reaction of events and circumstances that bring about the desired results. It's like you just got an injection of magic and luck into you life.

Tool for changing beliefs

How does one believe totally at will? This is a difficult question to answer because each person is different and has a different set of mental awareness's that creates many variables. Sometimes it just happens like the above case with the ace student or it can be like the other student that struggled. It can seem impossible--like so many people that struggle with making enough money. It is important to mention that even the seven-second rule described in an earlier chapter can fail if one has fear around the request. When there is struggle with changing a belief, there is a core issue one must first discover and recognize to be the issue that holds one back from making the desired change in one's beliefs. This core issue is most always the cause of the fear that can stop a person in their tracks before ever getting a change off the ground. So many people in life want so much to make a change, but they never seem to be able to do it. The unrevealed core issue is the reason or the problem here. It may also be that the soul is telling you that there is an issue that needs resolve before it will let you pass the stage you are presently at. It will take a deep probing of oneself on an inner level to find the issue and bring it to the surface. To do this one may try giving intent to your higher self to discover/reveal the issue; deep thought; meditation; talking over problems with a trusted friend; writing down one's thoughts, desires and problems; hypnosis, regression or even ritual to delve deeply enough to discover the issue. Ritual is another subject that is related to magic and its practice. We will discuss this shortly, but first there is one other topic to mention here, which is to ask for guidance on the issue while in a quiet place where you will not be disturbed. Get relaxed and ask for help from your guides, heaven, God, etc. It matters not which you choose here, it only matters that you are genuinely sincere in your request. This is essentially the same as giving intent as mentioned above.

Let's talk about magic for a moment. Magic is another way to surface an issue or to create a different belief in oneself. But you must first understand how magic works. Magic has a catch-22 to it, it only works if you belief in the magic. *No belief, no magic.* Let's investigate this. Magic uses the power of true belief. What this means is if you believe the magic will work, then it will. A magic ritual is performed in a way for a person to convince ones mind and subconscious to believe in the intent of the ceremony. It can take repetition for this to work, like seeing a TV commercial about a sponge you first thought was dumb, but after nine months of seeing this commercial, you start to think or believe there may be something special about this sponge. You start to believe the commercial. Magic works the same way. It's all a matter of what you are willing to truly believe. A physical performance of a magic ritual has the effect on the mind and subconscious to make it start to believe. The words and actions of rituals are meaningless otherwise. With true belief magic ritual is not even necessary.

Knowledge gives one diversity and power over one's life and surroundings. Knowledge brings positive change to one's consciousness and thus to one's life and overall happiness. Having doubts in yourself will tear you down and hold you back from succeeding. Trust and believe in yourself 100% and you will automatically do the right things in your life that will bring you all those subtle circumstances, which subsequently attract all the right things in life that you want.

[Ms. Alison addresses the class.]

Ms. Alison:
That ends this chapter. We see that belief is a powerful tool that we all have. What did the author believe about his time and the evolution of the future? Andrew, would you comment on this question?

Andrew:
Yes, Ms. Alison. I see that he was trying to show another way of human

existence and a way of *thinking outside the box* as he called it. I don't know if we would have gotten here or not if he or they did not make the changes they did, but we are here now and that is the most important thing. I agree that belief is extremely powerful because if we didn't believe in going on in life as a species, we would just cease to exist in a relatively short time. I think if we were to believe that we needed to trade by using money, we would recreate that in our lives again.

Ms. Alison:
Okay, Andrew, thank you. Who would like to make any comments on this chapter?

Sandra:
I would, Ms. Alison.

Ms. Alison:
All right, Sandra, go ahead.

Sandra:
What I see are the limitations of the mind. He speaks of the unlimited ability of the mind more like we know it today. I do see, however, how that must have been similar to the earlier comment about thinking- when-they-thought-the-world-was-flat type of thinking. I am sure we are still in boxes even today with the way we think. I'll bet future generations will be even more open than we are just as we are way more open in our thinking than they were back then. I agree that what one believes is what makes things real, like he said about that old movie *The Matrix* when Neo questioned about the blood in his mouth after returning from the Matrix.

My science studies of the civilizations that were found to be extremely ancient compared to their known history has shown that other civilizations on earth were even more technologically advanced than the money era civilization was, but most of them never got past the era of self-destruction. This means to me that the ones that blew themselves up were not as advanced emotionally as they may have thought they were.

Getting back to this chapter, the part about thinking things and knowing things is very important. I have an understanding of this for myself and I am sure it is different than Sara's, but still similar. In our time we all know that we can have anything we want or need without having to exchange something for it like money. We have this knowing because money no longer exists. We have a relaxed, higher understanding and because of this we have an innate security. I feel a *knowing* for myself in the way I like school. I know I will be here all the way to the end. I know I have no desire to travel until I finish school. I know that I will see the world. I do not know how I know this, I just know it. But thinking about changing other things that I am not so sure of is a bit different. For example, I have wanted to be the lead actor in the play I have been acting in for several years. No matter what I did, I was always passed over for that part, until I sat down and really gave the whole scenario some serious thought as to why I was being passed over all the time. After going over many different ideas, I found that I was afraid of the responsibility of being the lead actress. I also found that it would mean that I had to kiss the leading man that I really didn't want to kiss. Once I got this figured out, I released that fear and the next year they had me read for the part and I got it with ease~plus they also chose another leading man that I didn't mind kissing at all. So you see things always work out for the best when the issues are let go of. The author suggested that releasing an issue can be hard to do, but I found it quite easy once I decided to figure it out and do it.

Ms. Alison:
That was great, Sandra. Let's have someone else take the next section on money. Who will volunteer?

Brad:
I will, Ms. Alison.

Ms. Alison:
Brad, thank you. The floor is all yours.

Brad:
I understand money to be the root of all-evil as we have read and talked about so much. But beyond that, I see that it relates to the differences between the two medical students—the one who had the knowing belief and the other with an uncertain belief. What I mean is that money can create inferiority between people that is not necessary. I have seen kids in school who feel they are inferior to other smarter kids, which is a natural occurrence that comes with the minds of the kids. But on the other hand, money has created inferiority where it would not naturally be if there were no money involved. Then he talks about nobody helping others on our planet. I think we do help others all

the time today. But I see his point because even today we all help because we also expect to get something in return. We do our share and then we take the things that others have created so we can have all the good things of life.

He mentions the freedom that removal of money would create for people. I have to agree with this too. Because if I had to earn money in order to have all that my family has, it seems I would not have very much at all. First, I do not know too much about how much money I would need and, second, I do not perform that much service because of school. It seems they did a lot of work back then to earn their money. So it just seems that I would have a hard time, plus it might take a lot of time to get what I have in my life now. Money was a very big manipulator of people back then. We have already gone over the manipulation thing, so I think that's about it for this section and me.

Ms. Alison:
Brad, thank you. We have yet another section on belief and the perception of magic to cover. Who will take this one?

Jack:
I think I have to make some comments today, Ms. Alison.

Ms. Alison:
Well then, go right ahead and dive in Jack.

Jack:
The way I see it is the power of *truly* believing in something is somehow a knowing. I guess I mean, does anyone think God *or the all that is* created everything because He thought like the struggling student? No. He just knew He could period. So He did. For *the all that is* I think there was no issue like we have. After all He was, or is *the all that is*. I think we are all created equal and with the ability to do anything we want. But for those people back then, I can see how the pressures and drudgery of having to work all the time to make enough money to pay bills and feed themselves along with the lower understanding of the way things really worked could cause many issues in some or most of the people. We all know today of the fall in consciousness that happened eons ago that is still a part of even our minds today that we are all still evolving out of. Most of us today do not have all those money pressures, so our issues are very minor compared to theirs. He wrote a lot

about how to try to get past those issues; it seems that it was a difficult thing to do for many of them. Otherwise, I don't think he would have tried to write so many different things about issues.

Since the author was a forward thinking person, I will bet he was ridiculed, scorned and not taken seriously by friends and acquaintances at times for coming up with such a bold and unconventional idea as to do away with money. I'll also bet he was quite different from most other people of that era. He must have also been one of those sovereigns too.

Ms. Alison:
Yes, he was, I have read his autobiography, I found it on the world net when I was seeking class materials. It said he was much more than just a sovereign, but you will have to read some of his other books to learn about that because they do not pertain to history and the subject of this class as this one does.

Since I know we have all read the personal experience of the divine at the end of this book, I want to make some comments on this section before we close out of this book.

From reading this section I want those experiences all the time too. I believe I have experienced this or something like this in my life from time to time. It seems people today are more in tune with their inner selves and this kind of experience can and does happen to many people around the planet. My only understanding of this is the same one I always tell my classes, and that is that there must have been an opening in the usual chattering of the mind that is always trying to direct one's life, which can be quite frantic and scattered at times. This opening is what allowed his divine self to enter. It may also be that the frustration that was causing him such pain spurred his divine self to lead him to go to a movie where his divine self knew his mind would calm enough for his divine self to make the contact that it did. We understand that quieting this chatter is a peaceful situation. This is also what the yogis and monks have been trying to do all their lives. I can only call it a gift bestowed on the writer that directed him to stay on course and eventually write this book.

I will read to you the closing parts of this book now.
[Ms. Alison reads to the class.]

A personal experience of the divine

I wish to explain one of my given experiences of and from my divine self. One day after I got divorced and was having some struggles in the world with money and relationships, I decided to drop everything and go do something else. I was new to the Phoenix area and went to a movie because I was bored and fed up. I just wanted to escape. I went to an action sci-fi movie to keep my mind entertained. While I was there I got into the movie pretty well, in fact, so well that I forgot the troubles that I came with. When the movie was over, my mind was calm and I walked out to the parking lot and suddenly I noticed I felt really good and in a kind of bubble where everything seemed very different from before the movie: very crisp, clear, and perfect. I walked with great smoothness and ease as if I was gliding. I got into my truck and left, and as I drove down the road my truck seemed to have more power than it ever had and there was not one single bump in the road. I drove directly home, about three miles thru heavy traffic lights, and never had to stop at a single one. This was impossible on that street for that distance and for the amount of lights there are. I didn't notice some things until after I came out of the experience, but while I was in this bubble everything was perfect. Every single blade of grass or cactus was just right as it was. This experience was clearer, higher, and smoother than any state drugs can ever generate. I felt that I could have become the president of the United States in a week if I chose to do so. I knew everything and could do everything and anything I wanted to. I could have gotten into a 747 jet and flown it away and would know all there was to know about flying instantly, just by looking at the controls. This was no hallucination. You cannot ever explain an experience like this in words and you have to experience it to know what this is like. I still feel that when this consciousness returns again (this is called awakening) that I will be able to give this experience to others maybe through a simple touch or even a thought to show others a small glimpse of what it is like to be the same as one's divine higher self.

The above description may say to you that all is okay as it is. No, this is not so because you are *not yet* in that experience of your divine self. Instead, you are in the lower levels of the 3rd dimensional reality. That bubble was an experience of the 5th dimension where my divinity could merge with me in the physical. When one walks on earth in full divinity, all will be perfect for that individual. This experience was given at a time I was very down and struggling with life and with the many questions I had but there were no answers. The phrase that everything is okay as it is, is correct for the past and the time being, it pertains more to nature than to people, but change is coming soon that will make what we have now with all the oppression and greed obsolete. We will be moving into a new era of existence. This experience has happened to me several times in my life. This experience was like my divine self descending into my consciousness for a time.

I have gone back and forth about the hate and force on the system's side and the people that are as good as gold on the other side of the fence frequently. As much as I keep doing this, the good in people outweighs the bad things thrown at them. No matter how bad it gets, the people come out on top. We will win against the situations we have helped to create against ourselves sometime soon in our near future of existence.

To sum it up

As stated in the beginning of this book, this has been a slow progression from present-time facts on up to a future with more evolved people that do not use money, followed by a look back at a past or current era with a different perspective about the use of money. I ask you, the reader, what would life be like today if money was done away with in our society? Do you think it would be peaceful or chaotic? People will surprise us all when it happens. Just look at the 911 tragedies when people all over the world came together to help others on earth in some way. I am not saying a tragedy is required for people to come together, we just need to start thinking outside the box of the old ways and move on up the ladder of evolution by doing away with the situations we all face on a daily basis because we use this thing we call money. The situation is worse than you may think because, like the boiling frog, we don't see exactly where or what we have gotten ourselves into.

All this talk about money is for a very real reason. The heaviness and density of human consciousness has become so dark that we the people cannot see who we really are any more. We have come to such an understanding of control and leadership like a herd of mindless cows. We no longer speak out or stand up for our individual idealisms. There is an energy on the planet that seems to be keeping things growing at a heavier and more controlling pace. It is well past the time for the free souls of earth to break out of that line of thought and mass consciousness and move into a greater free abundance of life on a level never before done by humans. Getting rid of money is a huge step in the right direction toward true abundance for all humanity.

When it comes to your beliefs about money, or anything for that matter, one can use the tools and suggestion gleaned from this book and make the changes one needs if so desired to attract money into one's life.

This book, however, is not about attracting money into one's life. It is about getting rid of it for a better way of life that must start now. There is no spiritual key here for attracting money into one's life for today's people unless that is the desired intent of the reader.

Protector of souls

As a light-worker I too am on the path of enlightenment, after many years on this path I could be called a protector of souls of man. It could be said that I am one of the many in the physical to protect the souls of men through teaching the minds of men and once more helping others to remember our true origins of the soul. This remembrance will bring the required evolution of humanity back out of the darkness man has fallen into over the past few eons of time. When our origins are known again, we will return to the path of enlightenment as we were meant to be on all those many ages ago. We as a species have strayed far and long off the path of the *all that is*. We set out to experience the physical as a fragmented and highly reduced part or extension the "*all that is*" because the *all that is* could not reduce itself to the point of becoming physical. We split off so the *all that is* could see itself from a separated perspective. The *all that is* cannot see itself it can only see as we see ourselves from the inside out into the cosmos. By separating from the *all that is* by the will of the *all that is* we are the extensions of and subsequently are experiencing for the *all that is* in the lower dimensions of the creation which came from the *all that is* through our creation of the universe we exist in. We are a denser form of the *all that is*. We experience for the *all that is* what it cannot and then that experience is transferred back to the *all that is* so it may experience all of its creations, even down into the darkest parts of the great void. We are all a part of the whole. We are also distinct creations that have become in a sense separate from the *all that is* through our journey and evolutionary path. We are returning back to the whole but not in the sense of being absorbed into the *all that is* as if we never existed.

As children we are not always subject to the workings of light-workers on earth. After we have had a good dose of the earth plane at early adulthood we become strong enough in human existence to feel that it is our normal state of being. Then we are slowly subject to the workings of the higher realms and start to bring in the higher vibrations. This mixing of energies can have the effect of disorienting us because we are starting to exist in two worlds at the same time. At times we will need to be re-grounded to the earth plane by eating chocolate or meat or by intent to be grounded. This disorientation can be very disconcerting from time to time. It however is a normal part of the ascension process.

Authors closing comments

Reading this book shows you have a stirring of awareness of and restlessness about today's systems. The fact that you are reading this book shows that you are awakening to the need for change in our unjust, harsh reality of society. You have been led to this book, as there are no coincidences in life.

This book has been a primer for those of you who are not in touch with your true inner self. You are likely still sleep walking on earth. This should be obvious to you from reading this book and finding most or all the information in it as eye opening as it pertains to the laws of society and the higher awareness's available to you. Other shades of awareness that you may or may not be aware of on other levels deep within your psyche, mind, and soul have started to awaken in you. If at any time you felt goose bumps on your body from reading this book, your were getting a validation that the encoding process was happening and a truth was recognized by a deeper part of you. Even if you didn't get the goose bumps, you still got the encoding.

Hidden within and between the words and analogies of this book was an encoding of information that has changed your cellular makeup at the DNA level. The words have little meaning in relation to the encoding except that they are like a key to open a door that lets the encoding in. This will likely not even be noticeable to you. This was designed to bring you greater inner conscious awareness. Reading this book has genetically encoded your DNA and it will reawaken a part of you that has been long lost and forgotten. If you read this book and close it doing nothing with the information contained in it, you have still been encoded in a small way. You will genetically carry this encoding with you to the next lifetime where you will have a predisposition that will help the people of that time to change the world for the better. If you have children in this life after reading this book, the encoding will be carried over to them through your DNA. They may become society changers at an adult age to some degree. The point is that all information you read is taken in on some level and stored and used for your evolution as needed. You forget words at times but you cannot unlearn what you have learned, as it becomes a part of you forever. Everyone is on a path of evolution no matter what you may think. We all live, die, and return to live again. We are all constantly evolving. Each new life is another step on the cosmic path. This author has been told by higher sources that he will be one of the chosen to write some of the spiritual, informative books for the coming future generations.

A backup plan

The first steps of the reform of the money system are underway with the NESARA Act. This stands for National Economic Security and Reformation Act. This act will when it is implemented return the money system back to a GOLD standard backed money system and will close down the Federal Reserve and the IRS, the money will then be printed by the government instead of the private corporation known as the Federal Reserve, it will forgive all loans throughout the entire country, as well as other things that I will not list here.

In early 1993, the nine US Supreme Court judges ruled seven to two in favor of the farmers on all major issues including that the Federal Reserve Banking system was unconstitutional, that the US has been operating outside the Constitution since March 1933, that major reformations of government and our banking system are required, and that financial redress and remedies must be provided for financial losses due to bank fraud suffered by generations of Americans.

This is only one step toward an new system that will still use money but it will be at least better than the federal reserve note system, however the use of money only breeds corruption and power in the minds of men and would continue to be devastating to all of humanity as long as it is being used. This act is good as it reverts the money system back to what it was in the beginning of the united States but it will not cure the real problem at hand. The corruption of the soul dead people that walk this planet will continue to make their way into a deceitful existence as long as they have a way to gain control over others. That way is to continue to use and put our energy into money. The only real cure is to remove the money and you remove the temptation. Those souls will then turn to more peaceful ways of living and this will bring about an advanced state of evolution even for them.

Ms. Alison:
Well class that finishes the book. If there are no more comments, then we will finish here. No. Well then, class, I think we have covered enough of this book for this class. We will be going onto another book when we return tomorrow. Let's close now with these new understandings of this past era and hope it never comes around again for humans.

AND THEY ALL LIVED AND
EVOLVED HAPPILY EVER AFTER

THE END